The Woodturner's Workbook

The Woodturner's Workbook

Ray Key

B.T. Batsford Ltd · London

To my wife Liz and son Darren for their continued support, despite the fact that woodturning has almost become an obsession.

To all my fellow woodturners around the world whom I have had the pleasure of meeting and learning from. To those turners whose work is featured in this book. To Dale Nish and Nick Cook for allowing me to use photographs No 19 and No 81, which were taken by them. To Frank Boddy for allowing me to quote his thoughts on timber. To my editor Samantha Stead, who has worked so hard with me on this publication.

All photographs and drawings are by the author, as is all the work that is not credited.

The front cover illustrations show:
Top left: Burr oak log chain sawn into manageable sizes. Top right: Large wormy ash vessel (Dale Nish). Bottom left: Burr oak natural topped bowl (Ray Key). Bottom right: Delbergia (rosewood) boxes (Ray Key).

The back cover illustration shows two cherry bowls (Darren Key, aged 14).

First published 1992, reprinted 1994
© Ray Key, 1992

Typeset by Goodfellow & Egan Ltd, Cambridge
and printed in Singapore

Published by
B.T. Batsford Ltd
4 Fitzhardinge Street
London W1H 0AH

A catalogue record for this book is available from the British Library

ISBN 0 7134 6667 7

Contents

Introduction

Background

In recent years (particularly in the past twenty or so) woodturning has gained a new and vibrant impetus – this very ancient craft, with a history going back several thousand years, has blossomed. There is much turned wood being produced today that many perceive as art, and although this is something that often produces heated debate, since many consider woodturning as purely a craft, there are in my view many turners around today who have elevated their craft to a fine art. These woodturners have the ability to respond to wood sensitively and creatively, producing objects that allow their artistic talents to flourish.

Burr oak bowl 405 × 190 mm (16 × 7½ in)

The perception of woodturning as purely a craft is for the most part a somewhat historical one, for by and large the turner has been a maker of useful things over the centuries: things to eat and drink from, things to work with, constructional, industrial and architectural components, containers, furniture, toys – the list is endless. Artistic quality was very much of secondary importance, with function the priority, and although some work was aesthetically pleasing, much was not. One area where the woodturner did display his creative and artistic skills in the past was in artefacts for use in ceremony and ritual, but again use was the primary concern.

Recent years have seen a change. As wooden items used for utilitarian purposes have faced stiff competition from man-made materials such as plastic

and stainless steel, many turners have started to produce work that is strictly non-functional. There will always remain, I am sure, a good market for well made wooden tableware, as man-made materials can never give the same pleasure in use as natural materials. Wood in particular is especially warm and tactile. There can be only one winner when it comes to serving salad: the natural feel of a wooden bowl is so much more wonderful than that of cold, clinical stainless steel. Something may tell you that I am a wood lover!

The modern movement

Through much of the twentieth century the more traditional hand woodturner has seen his role decline. Much that was done by hand can now be done by automated machines, and the advent of new materials, often more durable than wood and cheaper to produce, has made life difficult. Despite this there are many who have survived by becoming either more versatile or more specialized in the work they undertake.

The past twenty years or so have witnessed a new interest in woodturning and an awareness of it as a creative medium. More leisure time, less job satisfaction, and more stressful living have all contributed. Throughout history man has been a creator and a maker, but as modern technology has removed much of our creative and manual dexterity, so it is only natural we should look for something to give us creative satisfaction. Woodturning offers this choice. Where modern society has created a very stressful environment for many in their work place, a workshop with a lathe often proves extremely therapeutic, a place where you can disappear into a world of your own and create objects that fill you with pleasure – and for me, so much so that I chose to make woodturning a full time living in 1973.

Despite what we may think, most people have more disposable income today, and the new-found interest in woodturning has fuelled a new industry. There are now suppliers throughout the world willing to supply you with lathes, tools, chucks, wood and books; in fact anything they think the turner might need. There have been many developments beneficial to us all. Sadly, there are also gadgets sold that you feel you can't live without, and only later do you find their use was confined to getting you to part with your hard-earned cash. Along with all this has come an increased thirst for knowledge,

and courses, workshops, seminars, books, are available in profusion: some good, some indifferent. National associations have been set up in many countries, linking turners in a way not seen before, and offering many services to members, all dedicated to creating greater technical and creative awareness, and raising standards.

There is a willingness worldwide to share the knowledge we have in a way that has never happened before. Gone for the most part is the guarded 'trade secret' brigade. Today most of us are willing to pass on our hard-won knowledge. It is my belief that this new willingness to impart information has fostered the new creative spirit found in contemporary woodturning. This is coupled to the fact that our consumer society demands visually creative and stimulating decorative objects to display in the home. This is an area where woodturning has got some catching up to do when compared with ceramics and glass, but progress is being made: more and more objects of artistic merit are being created, and demand is now growing through increased public awareness.

None of the recent developments has come about by accident; pioneering spirits have been crying out for recognition for years, mostly in the USA. It has been for the most part the USA that has nurtured this embryonic movement of creativity, and the subject matter that has captured the imagination of the makers, has been the vessel.

It was James Prestini, during the thirties, forties, and fifties, who elevated the humble wooden bowl from a purely utilitarian object to a work of art. For him purity of form was paramount: thin walls, with grain formations utilized for best effect, resulted in a refinement not previously associated with turned wooden bowls. Museums, private individuals, and corporate bodies across America have collected his work, recognizing his contribution to woodturning and the timeless quality his work displays.

From the forties until the present day, Bob Stocksdale and Rude Osolnik have been making bowls of the highest quality. Stocksdale uses exotic woods and creates elegant and delicate bowls the equal of any made in porcelain. Osolnik has had a more catholic approach – laminated plywood and natural-

Right: Rippled ash vessels from quarter sawn timber. These take twice as long to make as end-grain pieces. The largest is 153 mm (6 in) tall

topped bowls (he was making these in the forties) are his signature pieces. These three men, over the years, sowed many of the creative seeds from which the modern movement grew in the seventies.

In the seventies in Britain the crafts in general began to re-awaken public interest, and craft galleries, a new phenomenon, began to spring up. The gallery was looking for something different, something other than useful domestic wares (although these goods formed the backbone for most). The woodturner's response to this market opportunity was slower than that of many other craftsmen. But gradually there was a response, mostly from new turners who had given up jobs in education, the City, and industry. Their interest in the craft was fuelled mostly by articles written by Peter Child and Geoff Peters in *Woodworker* and *Practical Woodworking*, and the wonderful Frank Pain, in his book *The Practical Wood Turner*. These newcomers to the craft started to produce the type of work of interest to the galleries, while the more established turners remained working in their more traditional areas (although some did produce domestic ware for the galleries). Meanwhile, in the USA in the mid seventies, three significant things happened: *Fine Woodworking* magazine was launched, Al LeCoff started woodturning seminars, and Dale Nish's first book was published.

These events in my opinion formed the catalyst for the creative explosion that came and has continued ever since.

Aims

My main aim in writing this book is to stimulate a greater creative awareness of the potential of turned wood. All turners, whether hobbyists, amateurs, professionals, part-time, or full-time, need a stimulus from time to time – as one who earns his full time living from woodturning (eighty per cent from making) knows only too well. Through seminars and teaching I am in touch with many who are in search of this stimulus. Many are technically proficient and able to produce competent work, but what they seek

is that elusive element that they perceive will lift their work above the ordinary. Such an element is very difficult to define. What makes the perfect design? How does one acquire the knowledge and skills to achieve it? The answer will always be down to the individual. The majority of woodturners have no formal design or art training. There are exceptions of course, and many of the visually stimulating objects created in recent years have been made by those who have. But don't despair, there are just as many created by those who haven't had the training. I hope, in this book, to provide you with as many guidelines and touchstones as I can, to help you on the right track.

A sound understanding of balanced proportion and form is a good starting point. Observation with a keen eye will allow you to embark on an osmosis form of learning about proportion, scale, balance, form, detail, and style; all are elements with which you will have to come to terms. Once you have started to grasp some of the basics (it will take time)

you should be able to start creating designs of your own. If you are one of those fortunate people who has a good imagination and has grasped the design principles you will be well on your way to producing some good original work.

Those who find it difficult to be creative (and most do), although they have become competent in the making skills, often copy traditional and modern turners' work. To me this is quite understandable, and it can help you grasp some of the elements of good design, but there are many modern makers who find copying or plagiarism (call it what you will), a very vexed and emotive issue. I do not think that anyone really gets upset when someone makes the odd piece for their own pleasure; in fact, that may be perceived as flattery. It is only when people start to sell copied work on a regular basis that the originators get upset.

Remember, no copy ever has the integrity of an original. No copy is likely to be as good as the original, because the originator's conceptual spark is missing. So, try to develop your own ideas, and if you use those of others, please do not try to copy them faithfully; it does not work. However, it is quite

Laburnum shaped-top bowl with sapwood edge 152 × 90 mm (6 × 3½ in)

Boxes with chatter tool work in the lid. From left to right: *snakewood, pink ivory, Honduras rosewood. 50 mm (2 in) diameter*

possible that you may be able to find something in another's idea that gives you the basis to develop a range of shapes and forms of your own. I am quite often surprised to hear colleagues say it was the work of 'so-and-so' who inspired them, since there often seems little trace of that person's work in their own. What it means is, they have been able to put their own personal stamp on their work, even though it was inspired by someone else's pieces.

My own approach to the creative design process is variable, but decisive in execution; what I mean is that when I start to make any object I have a very good idea of what it will look like when it is finished. With experience you will build a repertoire of forms and shapes, and these will enable you to respond in sympathetic and positive ways to your material. Wood can be very seductive, and it is easy to fall under its spell, particularly when confronted with spectacular grain and figure. However, remember that these will tone down in time, and then it is the

form that becomes the dominant force, not the once-spectacular grain. Those who have the ability to exploit the full potential of the material and get the form right at the same time, will achieve the most consistently successful results. The repertoire of shapes you build for yourself should hopefully allow you to respond in a number of ways when confronted with similar pieces of wood. With experience you should know which of these shapes will or will not work when you look at the wood's grain configuration.

Observation of the world around us is where I personally derive most of my creative inspiration. Nature, buildings, street objects, industry, fashion, and the home, all give a good basis for creating designs. Many of my designs are born through the ability to translate my observations into objects that are distinctive, so that most people do not even realize what sparked the idea. None of them are copies, but are visual interpretations of my observations. In the course of this book I shall attempt to communicate this creative process, dealing with various themes and giving plenty of touchstones for design.

1
The material

1
The material

Wood and the environment

Wood is one of the world's greatest natural resources and one of our few renewable ones, a fact which may have led it to becoming one of the most abused. There are tremendous ecological problems at this time because of the widespread destruction of the tropical rainforests, and when this is combined with much of the developed world's production of chemical pollutants and harmful industrial processes, the result is a major threat to the world's environment.

There can be no doubt that something needs to be done, and fortunately positive steps are being taken: of course we are all being made aware of this need by the media and various environmental pressure groups. However, in the effort to create a reaction there has been in many cases an over-reaction, leaving the public, and especially craftspeople, confused.

There are no easy answers to what is a very complex issue. Some countries rely heavily on the sale of their timber for revenue and have managed their forests well. They have not resorted to slash-and-burn or clear felling operations, causing soil erosion and the creation of vast tracts of wasteland, but carry out selective felling and a replanting policy. It is unfortunate, then, that because of an over-reaction in some quarters these countries find their economy threatened, after doing everything right. We in the Western World can be said to be very hypocritical: after all, most of us live in homes where forests grew a few centuries ago. We felled our forests to grow food, raise cattle and build our homes – the very activities we are trying to stop in Third World countries today. Obviously the tropical rainforests are a totally different proposition from those that grew or grow in the temperate areas of the world, but it seems unjust to preach to people what we have clearly not practised ourselves.

I am not sure whether what is happening today is any different from what has been happening for centuries, except for its speed. The mechanical equipment used in timber felling and extraction today (just think what one man can do with a chain-saw) probably means that what used to take ten men a week to do can be done by one in a day. It is this pace that compounds the issue; in the past more selective felling and the slower rate meant that there was a constant regeneration.

The rainforest countries of the world must be encouraged to realize that forests are a valuable asset, and we in the West will have to pay a higher price if we want the timber. Timber should be seen as a crop and cultivated as such: when these countries are paid a decent price they will surely manage their forests properly. Well-managed forests should yield fine timber and a decent income for the producer for ever.

At present the public and the makers are in a quandary. Many customers will not buy goods made from any sort of imported wood, nor will some makers use it. This represents an over-reaction by both parties. Much wood that is imported into this country comes from well managed renewable sources. Remember, we are not self-sufficient in timber ourselves. There can be nothing wrong with a maker using imported timber if it comes from a renewable source of supply. (Do not forget that the purchase of this timber is providing much needed revenue for that underdeveloped country). Until now this has been difficult for the maker to guarantee, but there are now a number of suppliers willing and able to give this assurance. So seek that assurance from the supplier.

Perhaps some of the most interesting and considered thoughts I have seen from a timber merchant in recent times have come from Frank Boddy, a well known and responsible merchant. The words

Burr oak log chain sawn into manageable sizes, all end-sealed to retard splitting

that follow have been extracted from his latest mail order catalogue.

'On average no more than 10 per cent of the timber extracted from a tropical rainforest worldwide is put on the international market. 90 per cent is used or burnt in the country of origin. It should be noted that the UK directly imports only 0.93 per cent of the world's production of sawn tropical hardwoods and 0.03 per cent of tropical hardwood logs ... [it was] the UK Timber Federation who led the way to establish the International Tropical Timber Organisation [ITTO] which now has 50 member countries who have the united aim to conserve the tropical rainforests, which includes improving forest management and promoting the use of lesser known secondary species.'

Frank Boddy strongly supports the Timber Trades Federation 'Forests Forever' campaign and the target set by the ITTO that by the year 2000 all hardwoods being imported into member countries should be from areas of verified sustained resource.

'... This may mean we will all have to pay more for our hardwoods – a small sacrifice to make to preserve a major part of our ecology for future generations.

Forests and woodlands have a continuous natural process of change, as over mature trees die, young saplings grow to replace them. Harvesting mature trees as part of a planned replanting programme, combined with good forest management, facilitates timber being available as a market commodity whilst retaining natural forest or woodland. In addition lesser used secondary and exotic hardwood species need to be promoted to timber users to ensure timber volume remains constant in order to meet the growing demand for hardwoods.'

Frank makes the following points and plea:

'*I feel it is important that before any decision to boycott the use of tropical hardwoods is taken the impact of such a boycott should be fully considered. The rain forests provide badly needed revenue for Third World countries who are facing increasing problems. These include the necessity to reclaim land for farming, to grow food for their expanding populations, to clear land for industrial development and to create reservoirs for hydro electric schemes. This is not an exhaustive list of Third World countries' requirements for revenue. One of the ways forward is to utilize the hardwood rainforests as a community, which with well-planned harvesting and replanting pro-grammes need not destroy the rain forests but develop a continuing industry.'*

Frank's thoughts echo much of what I have been trying to say. As a maker I use both northern temperate and tropical hardwoods in my work, including small quantities of exotics (around 15 cubic feet (180 board feet) per year) as opposed to 300 cubic feet (3600 board feet) per year of northern temperate woods.

Top left: *Wonderful root structure of a beech tree as it fights for survival high in the Cotswold hills*

Bottom left: *A young fallen ash tree in the Smokey Mountains, which took many other young trees with it. Regeneration will take place as more light reaches the forest floor*

Below: *Burr maple wind-blown in gales. This was a tree I had long admired, but on inspection the burr was only sapwood deep*

2
Selected timbers

2
Selected timbers

In a publication of this nature it is only possible to give a brief insight into the properties of a relatively small number of timbers. What can be said is that every timber has its own very different characteristics. This is all part of its particular fascination, be it its colour, texture, grain, smell, strength, or working properties. Most of us will only come into contact with and work with a relatively small number of the seventy thousand woods of the world known to man. These woods range from scrub-like heathers to forest giants, and only around four hundred make up the world trade in timber. Few people will work more than fifty or so in their lifetime, and on a regular basis ten to twenty is a good norm. At this time my own count is just over one hundred, well above the average.

As a general comment it would be true to say that all woods can be turned, some with great difficulty, and others with ease. As I said above, every one has its own properties. Some I have worked leave me with no desire ever to do so again, while others I would happily work daily. Over the centuries various timbers have been found to have certain working properties which make them much sought-after for a particular use. For example, during the past two or three hundred years the names Cuban or Spanish mahogany (light to deep reddish brown), Rio rosewood (chocolate to violet-black), and walnut (grey-brown to dark brown with blackish stripes), have been synonymous with the finest furniture, and remain so today. However, now, through over-exploitation, these particular mahoganies and rosewood are virtually impossible to find on the world market, except in veneer form. Other less fine timbers, such as oak (light tan to biscuit, or rich deep brown (brown oak) or almost black (bog oak)), and Burma teak (golden brown) also have an association with furniture. But again, through over-exploitation, this particular teak has virtually disappeared. Yet although these timbers are much sought-after by furniture and cabinet makers, only Rio rosewood and walnut, I suggest, hold the same appeal for the headstock turner. The spindle turner will be happy to work them all.

Why is this? It is down to workability and fashion, in the main. The headstock turner always encounters great difficulty because in headstock turning the fibres of the wood are directly opposed to the axis of rotation of the wood, (something the spindle turner avoids as he always works with the grain) and in this respect oak and mahogany are particularly tricky to turn. Especially in bowls, tear out and a woolly surface texture are common. Walnut can also give these problems, but normally to a lesser degree. I would always choose Rio rosewood. Although it is oily and hard, it works well and takes a fine finish.

If you did not work with teak in the sixties and seventies (when almost every modern home was furnished with it) as a turner you were likely to starve. Burma teak always works well, being a naturally oily wood (teak from other countries often has silica deposits which take the edge off the tools instantly) but it has a strong pungent smell which can affect some people by causing a burning sensation at the back of the throat. Fashion has now changed, and teak has almost disappeared. Lighter woods such as pine and ash are now more fashionable, or alternatively jet black woods, often stained ash. It is difficult to gauge whether changes of fashion are always by design, or whether they are forced by the near extinction of a species that has been in vogue.

Fine work made from these household-name timbers will always find a home, though perhaps not as readily as when they were the height of fashion. But the very mention that a piece is made from walnut or rosewood brings an instant response from some people.

Two highly figured pieces of wood that have vastly different working properties. The disc is of quilted crotch Cotton wood: this is extremely difficult to work, where as the narrow length of quarter sawn London plane (lacewood) will work easily

As I have said, every timber has its own characteristics, but perhaps I should say that every *tree* has its own characteristics. The terrain, mineral deposits in the ground and climate where each tree grows all affect its structure, colour, and growth. General descriptions found in books on timber consist of those features most commonly found in a species. However, there will be a great deal of difference between one tree grown in a forest or prime woodland and a similar tree grown on poor subsoil on a hillside exposed to the elements in a colder climate. Something like a forest-grown ash tree will normally make fairly vigorous growth. Being drawn up to the light, it will have a straight stem of even growth. The first branch will break high up, the tree will be tall and elegant and sought-after for a multitude of uses. The grain will be fairly coarse but straight, as is the ash characteristic. By contrast, the hillside grown tree will make slow, misshapen, stubby uneven growth, and will often be gnarled, with branches breaking low down and at random – certainly not a tree to be sought-after in the usual way. The forest-grown tree will work easily, but will probably prove bland and predictable (ideal for production work), whereas the hillside one will have a tremendously varied growth pattern, be problematic to work as there will be a lot of tension wood, but at the end of the day will give potential for some very beautiful individual pieces. Many of the most interesting timbers for woodturners are hedgerow or hillside-grown in the Northern Hemisphere. You will not find a more gnarled and misshapen tree than an olive, but this is one of the most wonderful timbers you will ever turn. Its aromatic smell, workability and marbled figure are tremendous.

European woods

By and large the colour range moves from the almost pure white of holly through creams and light browns to the grey/brown/black of walnut. Along the way there are a number of timbers that defy this generalization: plum, for instance, can be pink to red; mulberry is yellow when first cut, (though ultra-violet light soon sends it brown); laburnum has a greeny to chocolate-brown hue, and of course there are others.

I like to use all the fruit woods. Cherry, apple, pear, plum and damson are silky and work readily. Sycamore and plane work well, and mulberry is probably one of the easiest woods you will ever turn. Ash and elm have a relatively coarse grain structure but usually work well, although elm can distort and move unpredictably. My choice European timbers (plus one from North Africa) would be boxwood, laburnum, olivewood, thuya, and yew. Thuya and yew are both classed as softwoods because they are evergreens, but they are denser and harder than many a so-called hardwood. I choose boxwood (pale yellow) for its ease of working, its silky nature, its ability to take fine detail, and its stability; laburnum (greeny to chocolate brown) for its working properties, its colour and the contrast between sapwood and heartwood which can be dramatically exploited; olivewood (cream/brown with black streaks) for the reasons already extolled; and thuya (golden-brown to orange-red) for its extreme beauty, the fact that it works and finishes well, is resinous and extremely aromatic (the root burr is what we use, which comes mostly from the Atlas Mountains of Morocco).

Yew (orange-brown, often with purple and mauve streaks) was the bowman of England's timber. It turns and finishes well, has a silky nature, and a narrow white sap that contrasts well with the heartwood. Care has to be taken when finishing, as it is susceptible to heat cracks on the end-grain.

Rainforest timber

Timbers from the tropical rain forests of the world display almost every colour we know, and their characteristics are far more wide-ranging. The softest and lightest hardwood is balsa, with a specific gravity of 0.16, while the very hard and heavy snakewood has a specific gravity of 1.30. In Europe the specific gravity of timbers ranges from about 0.40 through to 0.90. As the tropical rain forests of the world provide by far the greatest range of species, I will cover just a few of the better known and unusual. Everyone, I feel sure, has heard of rosewood and ebony, timbers which have been synonymous with quality woodwork for centuries. What most people do not realize is the wide range of colours and characteristics that exist in these families. What confuses things even more is that there are timbers being sold as rosewoods which are not (a marketing ploy?) and there are a number of true rosewoods that do not have rosewood in their common name. True rosewoods are all *Delbergias*. The wonderful Brazilian tulipwood (cream and pink/red variegated stripes) has a delicate fragrance when being worked. Cocobolo (variegated yellow/orange/red – the dramatic colours tone down to a deep mellow orange red) has dust like snuff (it makes me sneeze, at least). Dust extraction is a must, as it should be whenever you are working any wood. Honduras rosewood (pinkish/purple/brown, with the odd black stripe) is sweetly scented when being worked, and very stable. Kingwood (variegated deep violet and black) is very fine and lustrous, and another timber with a pleasant scent, perhaps the king of all the rosewoods. Rio rosewood (chocolate to violet-black) is the rosewood with the most grain character, making it at times incredibly beautiful, and sought-after. Indian rosewood (purple-brown to purple-black) has a fragrant smell, but is dusty, coarser grained than most, softer and lighter in weight. It does not finish as easily as the others. African blackwood (purple/brown/black), looks black, but has a narrow cream sapwood that gives tremendous contrast. It is slightly oily, fine grained, and is the favourite timber for woodwind instruments because of its resonance, stability and ability to take an exceptional finish. These are just a few of the true rosewoods but it would be true to say that all rosewoods are dense and heavy, turn and finish well. Indian is, in the main, the lightest and softest.

There are one or two that masquerade as rosewoods but are not. Mexican rosewood, also known as bocote, is a fine wood but a *Cordia*, (variegated yellow/brown stripes). It displays wonderful contrast

Top right: *Selection of Northern Temperate woods showing some of the colour range.* Left to right back row: *plum, lacewood, olive ash, burr yew.* Middle row: *rippled white ash, walnut, laburnum.* Foreground: *boxwood*

Bottom right: *Selection of Delbergias (rosewoods) showing some of the colour spectrum.* Left to right: *Brazilian tulipwood, cocobolo, Indian rosewood, African blackwood, kingwood.* Foreground: *Honduras rosewood*

when first worked but quickly tones down to medium-brown. It works easily, is slightly oily, finishes well, and has quite a pungent smell when being worked. Santos rosewood (not a rosewood, a *Machaerium*) is very similar in appearance to Rio/Brazilian and is often sold as a substitute. It turns and finishes well, and has a nice sap contrast. Be warned – the dust can cause severe skin irritation to some people. Again, there are others sold as rosewoods when they are not. Be careful – they are still fine timbers, but they are not *Delbergias*.

Most people think of ebony as black, but this really isn't true. Most ebonies are variegated with black and brown stripes, except for the much sought-after African ebony which *is* normally jet black. All true ebonies are *Diospyros*, the best-known, I suspect,

being Macassar and Indian, but we obtain ebony from many countries, including Indonesia, Papua New Guinea, Sri Lanka, Thailand, and West Africa. I find the variegated ebonies much more attractive than the sought-after jet black African – to me, when that is polished, it is featureless and has the look of plastic. Most ebonies work well, but often dustily. The dust can be a problem. The dust from Macassar can give a burning sensation around the mouth and eyes. Dust extraction, and preferably an Air Stream helmet as well, is a must. Ebonies finish excellently, and are hard, but can be very brittle and split easily.

All the woods I have mentioned so far are ones I have used and some are definite favourites. To conclude this section I will select four more wonderful woods which are not part of the above families but certainly deserve a mention. They are very different in their colours, working properties, and origins.

Woodturners chaff – and no, it wasn't created on the pole lathe

Pink ivory (pink to red) is from Southern Africa and one of the most expensive timbers in the world. It is wonderful to work, having many of the characteristics of boxwood with the added colour bonus. It takes a lustrous finish.

Satinwood (golden-yellow) from India and Sri Lanka often has a wonderful, mottled, roe-ribbon figure, and has a fragrance when being worked that always reminds me of coconut essence. It turns well and is extremely lustrous when finished.

Snakewood (red-brown with black speckles) from Central and Tropical South America, has the look of a snake skin, as the name implies. It is also known as letterwood and leopardwood. One of nature's unique creations, one of the heaviest of all timbers, snakewood is very expensive and prone to split, but works and finishes beautifully.

Ziricote (dark grey with black lines) from Mexico, has the figure of Rio rosewood, and darkens to the colour of macassar ebony – what a combination. It finishes well, working is relatively easy but extremely dusty, and shavings are difficult to obtain. Chippings and dust are more likely.

This brief look at some of the timbers of the world concentrates on those I have worked on a regular basis. I have made no mention of timbers from Australia and New Zealand, although I am well aware that some of nature's real treasures come from that part of the world. I have worked many of them, but not enough to comment on in depth – those are pleasures waiting to be explored still further.

3
Unlikely material and timber drying

3
Unlikely material and timber drying

What to look for

The woodturner who produces work which is primarily for visual effect rather than function, is able to use much material to which timber merchants and most other woodworkers would not give a second glance. Much that is discarded and burnt is the material which offers a rich seam for creativity. Small trees and branches, too small in diameter for normal commercial purposes, cancerous growths, knotted, decaying and worm-infested wood all provide a challenge for the maker to produce something that is unique.

Purposely omitted form this section are burr, (burl in USA) rippled, quilted, blistered, fiddleback, crotch and many other descriptions for well-figured woods, as these are much sought-after and highly prized, often for veneer, thus realizing high prices. (See chapter 4.)

I intend to outline a few suggestions for using materials that you may have previously felt were fit only for the fire. But before doing so a few tips on how to dry both your unlikely materials and more conventional woods could be useful to you.

Drying

Outside

All timber should be laid down on bearers, whether in log or board form: this will prevent contact with the ground, which can cause rot and decay. If the log has been converted into boards, place stickers (*thin strips of wood*) between each board, directly above one another. These should be slightly longer than the width of the board, spaced about 610 mm (24 in) apart. This will allow air to circulate, aiding the drying (this is the way most air dried timbers are seasoned). Sycamore is an exception and should be seasoned vertically to prevent discoloration.

The timber is best stored and covered with a sheet of tin or something similar, in a sheltered area away from direct sunlight and through-draughts, as these will dry the timber far too quickly from the outside, inducing splitting. Remember, when you take the timber inside it will still possess far too high a moisture content (around 16 per cent at best). Centrally heated homes have a moisture content of less than 10 per cent, so further drying time indoors will be called for. Keep the timber away from direct heat or extremely arid environments; one which is pleasantly warm with a reasonable humidity will be best.

Inside

Drying rules are similar: stand the timber vertically or lay it down on bearers. There is no need to cover it with tin; and if dry, the stickers can be disregarded. The rest of the rules are much the same; no direct sunlight or through-draughts, and a cool dry environment with no dramatic changes of condition should allow for a steady progressive drying to take place. I have been able to dry a log of boxwood up to 200 mm (8 in) diameter in this way, and yes, luck does have a part to play.

Burying

Place small logs in a pit 610 mm (24 in) deep on a bed of dry sawdust, with a 100 mm (4 in) layer of sawdust between subsequent layers of logs. This is a proven method of dealing with boxwood: the wood dries without loss of colour and with minimal cracking or shrinkage, but it does take time.

Boiling

This is a forced sap removal method in water, an adaption of the old method of laying logs in streams and rivers, allowing the water flow to drive the sap out through the timber's vessels. If you want to give this method a try, rough turn the wood close to the shape you have in mind for the object. Immerse it in cold water and boil; trial and error with different timbers and wall thicknesses will dictate the time required for this process. Wash under a cold tap, weigh periodically, store and dry in a reasonably warm environment. There will be some colour loss, but distortion and splitting will be minimal, once you have worked out what suits each timber.

Microwaving

This is something of a recent phenomenon. If you wish to hasten the drying time prior to completing the piece in a dry seasoned condition, once again rough turn the object. A wall thickness not greater than 25 mm (1 in) should give you a reasonable chance of success. Trial and error are again the order of the day. Alternatively you could turn your object from start to finish from wet wood and finally dry it in the microwave; you can even manipulate the shape, as the wood is extremely pliable when first removed from the oven. The oven should be set on de-frost.

PEG (Poly Ethylene Glycol)

This product is very useful for preventing splitting and distortion in any timber. I would recommend using this solution when you are using timbers that would normally not be used, or using them in such a way that splitting and distortion are the norm. For example, all log sections, large or small, with the pith core remaining, tension-growth timber, areas that have knots and so on, can all give problems. If, however, you rough turn to shape any piece of work from wet timber, immerse it in PEG of the correctly concentrated solution, and keep it at a temperature that allows it to work effectively, you should eliminate a lot of problems. The PEG replaces the sap in the vessels through osmosis absorption displacement, thus preventing shrinkage and distortion. The effect on the wood is dramatic: it cuts far more easily, because the timber's pores are filled with the PEG, which gives a waxy feel. The timber has, to a degree, become plasticized, and non-absorbent. It does have drawbacks: when you are finishing an object PEG clogs the abrasive quickly, so it is best to

Ash salad bowls rough turned and stacked to dry

finish with a polyurethane-based product. Any moisture or dampness in the environment will result in the finished object feeling like a bar of soap, clammy to the touch, unless you apply a finish that is impervious to moisture.

Dehumidifying chambers

These are very effective in hastening the drying of wood under controlled conditions. Many wood-turners use them. Normally a thirty to forty-five day cycle for drying is employed depending on the moisture content and thickness of the wood. A number of turners I know rough turn their work prior to the kilning process, often spraying the work with a hose pipe to ensure an even moisture, which in turn helps to ensure an even drying process.

Drying in thick brown paper sacks

This method is not quick but often works. After rough turning, put the work inside the paper sack, then remove it periodically and place it in another dry one, turning original sack inside out to dry. This method will prevent mildew and mould forming on the work.

Rough turning and drying slowly

This is my personally preferred method; I like to rough turn my work in the autumn and winter when the temperature is low, and let things dry slowly. The process takes place indoors in a dry environment that is not over-warm (9–12°C (48–54°F)), to allow slow sap evaporation to take place; this minimizes shrinkage and the tendency to split. If I wish to hasten the process, I have an old metal single bedstead that has a 0.75 kw, 1830 mm (72 in) greenhouse heater tube placed beneath it. Careful stacking and sticking of the objects results in very successful drying. I coat any suspect area in the timber with wax, or end seal it to retard the drying.

Wet turning from start to finish

You need to turn the piece of work extremely thinly for satisfactory results, and you must create the work very quickly, or distortion will take place while it is still on the lathe prior to sanding. A wall thickness of 3 to 5 mm ($\frac{1}{8}$ to $\frac{3}{16}$ in) or thinner will ensure the best results.

Whatever method of timber drying you try, remember there is a risk factor: it is not an exact science, so be prepared for a fair number of failures along the way. As your knowledge and understanding of wood accumulate, and with the help of a little luck, your chances of success will increase.

Branch wood and small logs

In every complete section of trunk or branch of tree you will find a pith core, heartwood, sapwood, the cambium layer, and bark. There will also be a natural split radiating from the pith core. If you are turning branch wood the split needs to be of the absolute minimum; it will also be best if the pith is as central as possible, which minimizes tension splits in drying. Drying such sections with minimal splitting is always difficult, and is an area that fuels endless questions and debate.

Here are a few thoughts that should help you on the way to reasonable success, if you couple them with the drying methods above. Timber selection is important: the slow-grown, dense hardwoods such as yew, box and laburnum (birch is a favourite in Scandinavian countries where much branch work is made) offer a higher success rate. So too will timber cut in the autumn and left in the longest possible lengths. If you are going to try seasoning naturally, seal the ends with wax or an oil-based product. Disregard any piece with a large split or a number of radial splits, since the chance of any seasoning success will be minimal. Much work produced from branch wood tends to be of the cheap giftware variety, but with imagination and skill, works of gallery standard are possible.

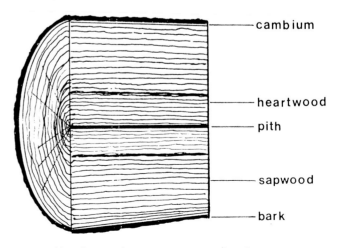

Section of log showing the main components of timber

*Work from small branch wood. Yew vase by Soren Berger;
laburnum grass vase by Ray Key; boxwood flower by Del Stubbs*

Spalted woods

Spalted (also known as dotty) timber has found much favour with woodturners in recent years, primarily for making eye-catching non-functional pieces. Spalting, in the very simplest terms, is caused by air-borne spores of fungi attacking the wood, and under the right conditions (usually humid) incipient decay starts. The typical black or brown ink-like lines that give the material its dramatic effects are called zone lines, which are created when two different fungi meet – in effect it is a battle demarcation zone. The effect on the wood is dramatic. This is the start of progressive decay, which often results in total decomposition once it is very advanced. However what is suitable for turning is material that has remained sound, but still has the dramatic effects caused by the fungi. This is seldom found, because various stages of attack and decay take place simultaneously within the material, since it is usually invaded by many different fungi, working at different speeds. When you come to work the timber you will find that while it is sound in some areas, it is punky or corky in others as the fibres decompose, which makes working the timber difficult. You have therefore to develop ways of dealing with it. The following are thoughts and ideas that may help, and are those I often employ.

Minor decay

Turn your work, using very sharp tools, close to the finished shape you have in mind, taking care that decayed areas have not torn or crumbled too much. Paint on several coats of a thin sealer that is either shellac or cellulose based: the wood will absorb it like blotting paper. By impregnating the decaying fibres like this, you will be able to cut them more cleanly when the sealer is dry.

Advanced decay

Normally it is best to disregard this material altogether, but if there are localized areas in a spectacular piece of wood, you can impregnate and strengthen it by using cyano-acrylic glue, the best being *Hot Stuff*. These glues are quite costly, so make sure the work is worth your investment. Hot Stuff comes in three consistencies, which resemble water, syrup, or honey. The water-like one gives the most penetration and is the one to use in this situation.

The syrup-like one penetrates slightly (1–2 mm ($\frac{1}{16}$ in)), and is ideal for suspending the fibres prior to making the final cut. The honey-like one has very little penetration, but can be useful as an aid to sanding.

31

Wonderful spalted beech log

Finished work in spalted beech

Sanding

Since there may be different stages of decay present, sanding can cause great problems because the softer areas will abrade more quickly, giving an uneven, pitted and rutted finish. If you use one of the methods described above you should have a more consistent density of surface to sand. Prior to sanding I always paint on a couple of thin coats of shellac or cellulose sealer on all surfaces, to stop the black/brown dust from the fungal zone lines impregnating the lighter areas, which would give the piece a very dirty and lifeless finish.

Safety

Take great care when working spalted woods. When wet the spores are often still active and pose a great health risk. This is lessened when the wood is dry, but at no time should you work this material without good dust extraction from the workshop or the use of a respirator safety helmet. I use them both simultaneously.

Timbers

All timbers will spalt given the right conditions, but for the most part the lighter woods give the best effects. In Britain, beech is the most consistent, while ash, chestnut, maple, can all be good. In the USA light woods such as beech, maples, birches, and fruit woods are all good, and likewise in Scandinavia where birch predominates.

Rotten wood

You can often use this for dramatic effect, usually by removing the rotted decomposed material and exposing natural effects that are difficult for man to create. Rot starts from the pith core or from the sapwood, so the removal of this decomposed material leaves you free to respond in the way you think most fitting.

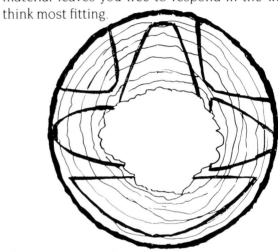

Above: *A large rotten-hearted log still has much potential for bowls*

Below: *Rotten-hearted burr boxwood log, and what can be done with it*

Beetle-attacked woods

Most timber is susceptible to attack from the larvae of beetles that lay their eggs in wood. The hatched larvae feed on the sapwood, leaving it riddled with holes full of frass. From the small common furniture beetle (woodworm) to the large powder-post beetle, they all create a network of tunnels in the sapwood. It is normal to burn and disregard such wood but the imaginative turner may put it to use. The frass needs to be removed from the holes to highlight the effect – though poking it out with a pin, nail or drill can be a laborious business. The finished object is best

Large wormy ash vessel by Dale Nish, end-grain turned

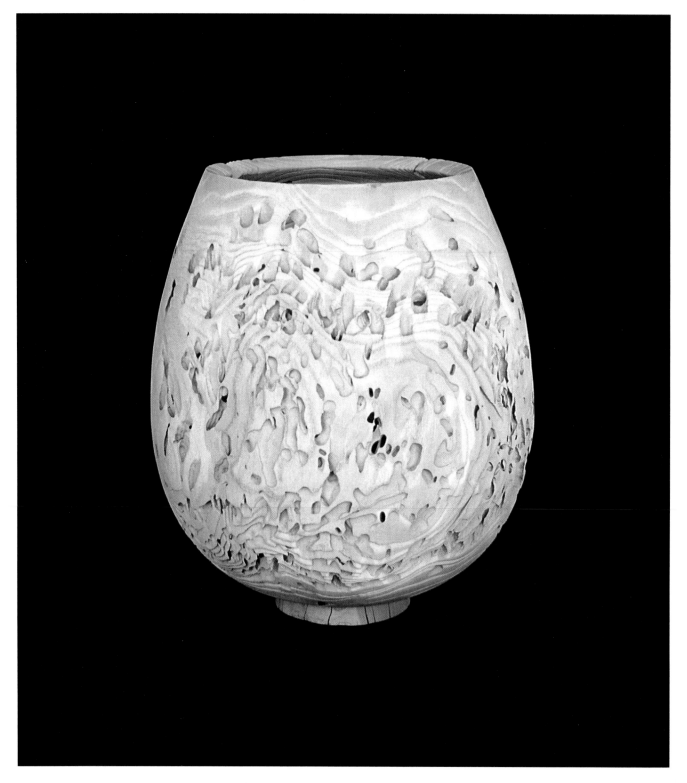

Novelty materials. From left to right: *banksia cone work by Ray Key, xanthorea root work by Jules Tattershall, tagua nut work by Dave Hout and Clead Christiansen*

given a shot in the microwave to kill any larvae that may still remain. If you do not, you may have an irate customer back on your doorstep. I suppose you could tell them it was a living piece, but rather you than me!

The most dramatic work I have seen using wood that has been attacked by beetle larva is that by Dale Nish. The green ash borer loves freshly felled ash, in Utah particularly, it would seem, and makes a network of tunnels around 6–8 mm ($\frac{1}{4}$–$\frac{3}{8}$ in) in diameter. The frass and the fat larvae make the turning of such material most unpleasant. A face shield and protective wipe-down clothing are essential. After turning, the objects are subjected to sand blasting, which removes the rest of the larvae and frass, and also erodes the soft summer growth wood, to create a weathered-looking finish. Dale tells me that wood that has been subjected to two years' boring gives the best effects; one year's boring does not yield enough holes, and with three years' boring there's not much left.

Novelty material

Xanthorrhaea (also known as blackboy and grass tree). This Western Australian material has found much favour in Britain in recent years. It is not a timber at all, but a root from the lily family. It is soft and fibrous, and best turned wet as it becomes very dusty when dry. Many turners have made very fine work from it.

Banksia-nut. Another unusual natural product from Western Australia. There is a large family of banksia trees, but only one produces a nut or cone that is commercially viable for the turner. It offers a number of possibilities for items of novelty. Pomanders are a favourite: if you hollow out the core and remove the seed pods, the scent from the pot-pourri passes through.

Tagua nut. This comes from South America – it is the dried fruit of a palm tree and is known as vegetable ivory. The colour and working properties are similar to animal ivory, but as it is only small, it is used for jewellery, very small turnings and inlays.

4
Sought-after materials

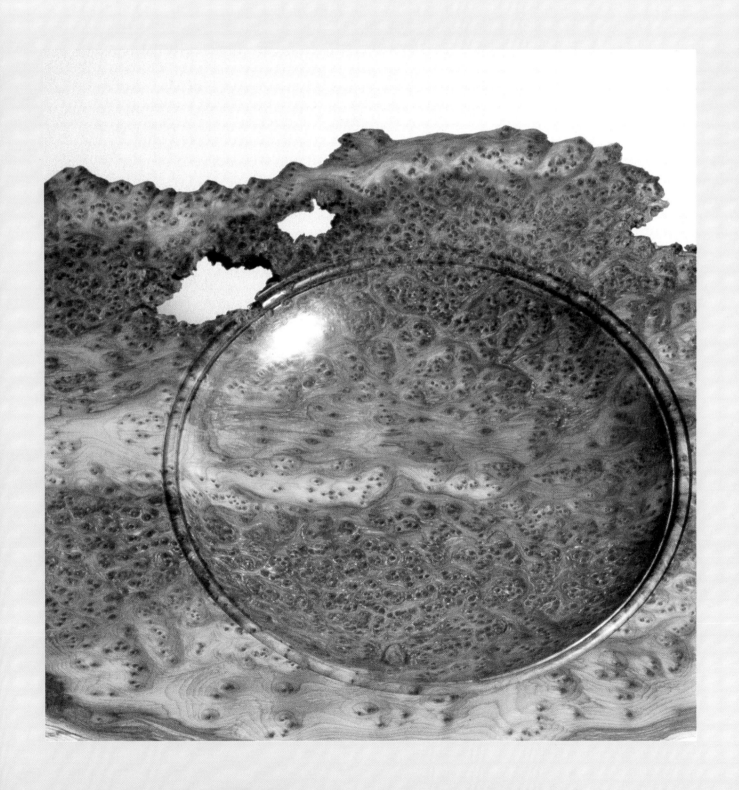

4
Sought-after materials

Wood is one of the most visually beautiful, warm and tactile materials in the world, and when it is highly figured with exceptional grain configurations, it becomes highly sought-after and prized by the veneer trade. Most of the best logs are slice veneer cut so as to obtain the finest visual effect, and, cut correctly, the material yields incredible prices, being used mostly for the finest furniture or for dramatic interior fittings, and panelling, and so on. However, there is much fine wood that doesn't find its way to the veneer mill for a whole multitude of reasons, and timber merchants, country sawmills, specialist suppliers, tree surgeons and all manner of other people have available, from time to time, an exceptional log or unusual piece of wood. On visits to your suppliers keep your eyes peeled, as you can often find some treasure in the most unlikely places. If you are able to build up a rapport with a supplier and he notes your interest, he will often give you a call the next time he has something he thinks may interest you. The types of grain figures that arouse the most interest are burr (burl), crotch, rippled, quilted, blistered and fiddleback. Of course, there are many others, but here I shall simply highlight these.

It would be true to say that for the woodturner wishing to display the full figure of many of these exceptionally figured woods with the minimum of waste, shallow dishes and platters offer the best opportunity. However, design-wise, this can be very limiting. In centuries gone by much emphasis was placed by the bowl turner on creating nests of bowls, to minimize the waste of any material, be it fine or ordinary. This process had a limiting effect on design likewise, and for many years this practice largely stopped, but now, though through new tool developments, many of us do remove a number of progressively smaller cores from extremely fine and valuable timbers. This allows for the creation of smaller but no less beautiful objects, from what would otherwise have been shavings on the floor.

Of course there are some cases where it will not be possible to save a great deal of material: the hollow enclosed vessel is one example.

It is my view that it is up to the user of these fine materials to create objects worthy of their use. Unfortunately, far too much work is being offered for sale today that relies totally on the wood's beauty. In time, as ultra-violet light and handling take their toll, dimming the material's once striking appearance, it is the shape and quality of the created image that then become dominant. Therefore, it is important that you acquire the skills to allow you to create objects of beautiful form. I have no hesitation in urging self-restraint on those of you who have yet to acquire those skills. I would strongly recommend that you use more ordinary materials until you have mastered both the technical and design skills required; only then will you be in a position to do justice to the more exotic materials.

It would be true to say that many of the most visually beautiful timbers are more difficult to work, another reason for restraint.

Fiddleback and rippled

Materials that display this figure often have the name 'curly' bestowed on them. Many trees exhibit this characteristic, but the sycamore/maple is perhaps the one that most people know of. It is the preferred timber for the backs of violins, hence the name 'fiddleback'. I personally use the term 'fiddleback' only when the undulating lines of grain are very close together. When they are a little wider apart I apply the term 'rippled'. This grain formation is caused when the normally straight longitudinal cell structure develops a wave in its growth.

Working the wood is sometimes difficult. There is a tendency with some species for areas to peck out. Sharp tools are essential and sometimes even then

Rippled olive ash platter, 500 mm (19¾ in) diameter

they have to be used in somewhat unorthodox ways, often testing to the full the technical skills of the maker.

Quilted

This description tends to be applied to timbers that have a more pronounced bulge form of growth than those displayed in fiddleback. When cut through, a more elongated figure emerges, which is often quite widely spaced, giving rise to its name. When a piece is tilted through different angles with a light source shining on it, the figure appears to roll up or across the surface. The working properties are very similar to those of fiddleback.

Crotch

The best crotch figure normally comes from the point where a tree forks, forming two equally tensioned stems that give a vee image when cut through correctly. The area close to the double heart often displays a dramatic feathered figure caused by tension or compression. Another area that will yield a crotch figure if cut correctly is the point where any branch breaks out from the tree trunk or from another limb. Here the tension and compression will not be equal, and the feather figure is not normally found; however the wood will still be very interesting and dramatically figured.

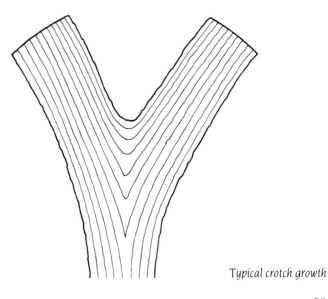

Typical crotch growth

39

Birdseye

'Birdseye' is a term used almost exclusively to describe the figure often found in American hard maple. There are several theories about what causes this unique figure. The one that attracts most favour is that, due to small conical growth depressions forming in the early growth of the outer annual rings, all subsequent growth seems to follow the same contour. The result is that when the timber is plain-sawn or rotary veneer-peeled, small concentric circles appear that give the bird's eye effect. The only other timber I have seen with this effect was a rare log of Zebrano.

Burrs (burls)

Much sought-after by all woodworkers but particularly by woodturners, the figure in these growths is perhaps the most eye-catching of all. The figures in most temperate woods such as oak and elm have the apperance of dormant pin knots caused by

Quilted grain of paldao

dormant bud formations, and in timber from some countries a marbled or pebble-like appearance predominates. What you can be sure of is that the formations will be variable, often contorted and gnarled, but of great beauty. There is much theoretical speculation about what causes this malformation of the tree's growth. Whatever the cause, the visual appearance on the tree manifests itself through an abnormal excrescence. The extent to which this happens is variable in the extreme: in some timbers it is just in the root; in others just a small local area on the trunk or on a branch; and in the ultimate case the complete trunk is covered from top to bottom. Often the burr (burl) figure is confined to the outgrowth from the trunk or branch, but the most sought-after and the best penetrate deep into the main body of the tree. My best find to date was an oak log totally burred from top to bottom, with a complete ringed blister growth; it measured 1525 mm (60 in) across at the base. The burr (burl) growth penetrated or radiated, depending on how you perceived it, to a depth of more than 610 mm (24 in) in this area, leaving only a 305 mm (12 in) central core unaffected by burr (burl) growth. A rare

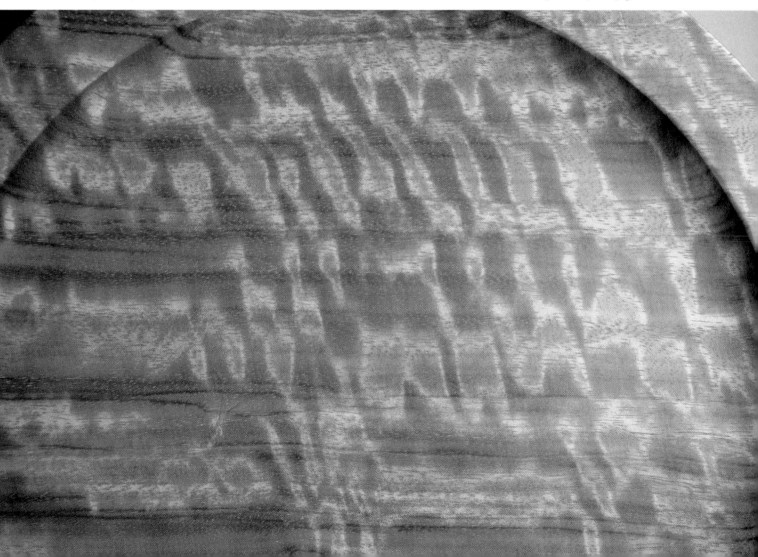

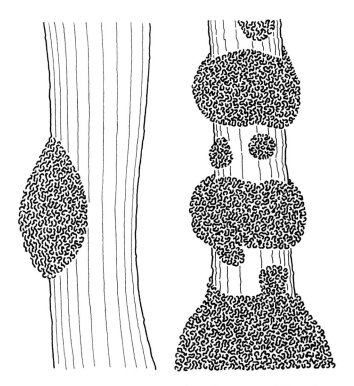

Left: *Typical side of tree burr growth.* Right: *Rare total blister burr growth. I once acquired a large burr oak log like this, 1525 mm (60 in) diameter*

find indeed. These growths provide the woodturner with a rich seam to exploit, and many opportunities for a display of true creativity.

Mazur

This term is reserved exclusively for an effect found in birch, normally from Scandinavia. The grain malformation is caused by beetle larvae; the cambium layer grows round the larvae and creates a unique flecked apperance. I have found an odd localized pocket or two exhibiting a very similar appearance in the occasional large white ash log.

The above is simply a very brief insight into some of the very spectacular figured woods that are so exciting for the creative woodturner. But the list is by no means exhaustive, as there are many other unusually figured woods – go out and discover them!

Below: *Burr yew dish, 482 × 382 mm (19 × 15 in). It is very rare to find this quality in yew*

5
Finishes

5
Finishes

Turned wood has traditionally been turned and sanded smooth, ready for the maker's selected finish. This is still the case for more than ninety per cent of the work produced today. However, as turning has become more sculptural and individual, many other finishes and practices have been developed. It is certainly worth exploring all the options, and fun to experiment.

Unusual finishes

Sand blasting

Sand blasting erodes the softer spring/summer growth on coarse-grained timbers such as ash, leaving a surface that looks weathered, rather like driftwood. This method was pioneered by Dale Nish and is now becoming quite common practice.

Chain saw

The use of the chain saw to give a rough, rugged look to turned wood is now much in evidence. It is often used as a contrast to a more traditionally prepared smooth and polished surface. Mark Lindquist was the pioneering force in this field.

Wire brush

Abrading surfaces with a hand-held wire brush, or a rotary wire brush in an electric drill, is a method being used by many to give a roughened surface and to erode some of the softer spring/summer growth.

Burning

Burning with a blow lamp or blow torch is another method that has found much favour with some turners. A black weathered surface is created as the softer spring/summer growth is burnt away, and when used on burrs, an ancient-beaten-metal effect is created. Jim Partridge was the first I am aware of to use this finish.

Microwave oven

Microwaves (set on de-frost) are often used when wood is turned wet. Objects placed in a microwave become very pliable and can be manipulated into many shapes that will stay in this form as the material dries and cools.

Bleaching, liming, and pickling in sulphates

These are other methods used by woodturners trying to give that added dimension to their work. None of these finishes is suitable for usable everyday objects, but some could be used to highlight an odd feature here and there.

Traditional finishes

Traditionally, many everyday objects had no finish applied, but we have been using wax, oil, and French polish, for centuries. In Scandinavia, Russia and much of Europe paint and dyes have been used for just as long. We now have a vast selection of products in each of these categories, plus a few others added for good measure, such as cellulose and polyurethane. There are so many products available that it is not surprising that people often make the wrong choice when finishing their work. What to use, how and when, are recurring problems in woodturning, and a great deal of good work is spoilt by poor and inappropriate finishes. Let me give you a few pointers. I should point out that I like wood to look like wood, which means I do not like high gloss finishes. To me they give the effect of a plastic-film barrier. My preferred finishes range from burnished matt to sheens of soft satin.

Oil

Clear teak oil (a refined liquid paraffin) provides an instant, usable finish, which is odourless and safe to use on all domestic, everyday, utility items. You need a liberal application, burnished friction-dry with soft shavings on the lathe. You will normally need to wipe corn or a vegetable oil on the piece periodically to keep it in good order.

Many oils that impregnate the wood make it almost impervious to moisture. Most have driers in them, give off an odour that takes time to evaporate, and often need a number of coats to build the finish. All this slows production, so bear that in mind if you do not want to spend too long on the finish. The finish, however, is excellent.

Shellac

Shellac is the base for traditional French polish and would have been used to finish much of the turner's work in times gone by. It is not used as much today for turned pieces because it is not a durable finish compared to many. I use a shellac-based sealer on some of the more open-grained timbers such as elm and oak, which are items of work I think will be used sparingly. It is best to cut back the sealer with fine abrasive, removing up to ninety per cent of the sealer, since you need only seal the open pores which would collect dust if left untreated. Apply oil or wax and burnish to a low satin lustre.

Cellulose

I use a thin, clear, satin cellulose lacquer on decorative work that I feel will be handled and admired. This stops finger marking and leaves the piece looking good without the plastic effect that many lacquers create.

Wax

My finishing wax is Toluene-based and is applied direct to small pieces of work made from very dense woods, or pieces that have been sealed with cellulose and flatted back. The dense woods I refer to are the ebonies and rosewoods; often if a sealer is applied to timbers of this nature a skin-like barrier is formed, taking away some of the timber's natural beauty.

Of course, I could mention many, many more finishing materials, but this is just a taster: never be afraid to explore the other options.

Burr oak bowl, shellac sealed and oil finished; and Santos rosewood bowl, cellulose sealed and Toluene waxed

6
Design

6
Design

Now we come to the crux of this book, and before I move on to specific types of object, and the touchstones by which you can judge your own creations and spark off new ideas, I would like to look generally at what I consider to be the important elements of design, and how I tackle them. Throughout the following sections I use particular terms and phrases, and perhaps it is worth explaining what I mean here.

Refined detail: For example, something like a bead, that gives the appearance of being applied to the surface of a flange. To be refined, it should be evenly rounded, the proportion of width and height equal, as should the depth of the step either side of it. It should not dominate but be in proportion to the piece as a whole. Small beads of this nature are best formed on close grained timbers that hold good detail, not coarse open-grained ones.

Subtlety: Smooth progressive fluid changes of surface, rather than abrupt, uneven, broken, directional changes.

Restraint: For example, the use of one line only when you might be tempted to make two. If in doubt, leave it out, especially on highly figured pieces.

Simplicity: This goes hand in hand with the idea of restraint, but I tend to use this term for practical items; fussy detail makes things difficult to clean and adds making time, so keep it simple.

Proportion

In each section I have outlined a proportional diameter-to-thickness guide, though of course increases and decreases have to be made for the relative design elements within a piece (eg. if you have 30 mm ($1\frac{3}{16}$ in) wide flange × 4 mm ($\frac{3}{16}$ in) thick on a 305 mm (12 in) platter or dish this will need to increase proportionally for larger ones of similar design – I might suggest 45 mm ($1\frac{3}{4}$ in) × 6 mm ($\frac{1}{4}$ in) for a 458 mm (18 in) one). Many other widths and thicknesses will work, of course, much depends on your design objectives.

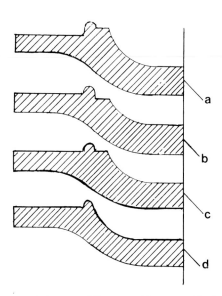

Bead treatments: (a) wrong; (b) wrong; (c) correct; (d) alternative

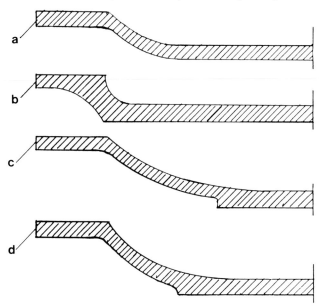

Bases of platters and dishes: (a) and (c) have the most life, while (b) and (d) are very stable, but lifeless

The bases of platters and dishes are usually of very different proportions. A platter usually sits on a flat base, which is often between half and three-quarters of the overall diameter. With a dish it is usual to have a foot ring that lifts the piece, this normally being between slightly less than a third and not bigger than two fifths of the overall diameter. Anything smaller or larger will result in something that is either unstable or lifeless.

One of the greatest challenges in designing is getting the proportions right, and although in each section there are specific guidelines and examples of balanced proportions, according to the object in question, this is the area where most mistakes occur. The following is certainly worth bearing in mind if you want to avoid the common faults.

Balanced proportion is essential, but easy to get wrong, so these thoughts are designed to try to help you not to fall into some of the many traps that await you.

Any feature such as a knob, a finial, a bead, or a flange should not dominate or be too small: each must be in keeping with the overall size of the object. A 25 mm (1 in) diameter finial on 102 mm (4 in) high × 50 mm (2 in) diameter box would be totally dominant, just as a 13 mm ($\frac{1}{2}$ in) diameter finial would be totally inadequate.

Any feature, be it incised lines, rounded edges, grooves, quilted effects or buttons, must all remain in proportion. A 13 mm ($\frac{1}{2}$ in) wide and 3 mm ($\frac{1}{4}$ in) deep groove near the edge of a flat-topped lid some 50 mm (2 in) in diameter, is far too dominant, but make it less wide and less deep and it becomes proportionally acceptable.

Any projections from the side of a lid, such as a lip, or bead, or flange, must seem to grow from the main body shape. The eye should be able to follow the main contour through without interruption. What I mean by this, is that if the feature were removed, the surfaces would continue to flow through without the lid being stepped in or out of line; if this happens the lid either is too dominant or too small. The drawings are designed to illustrate my meaning. I

Burr oak dish with natural edge

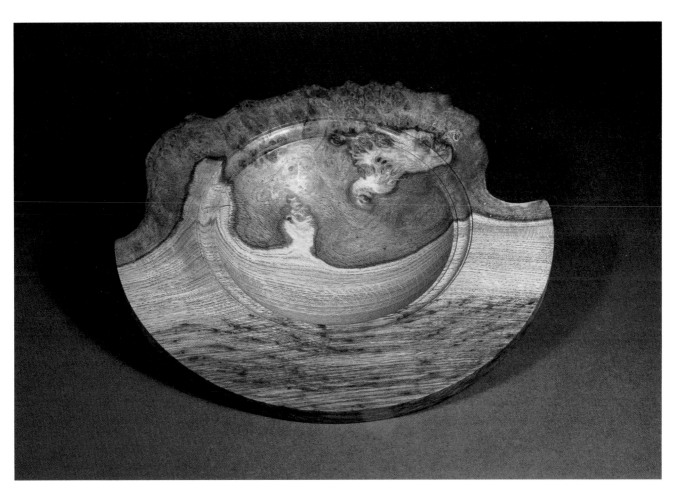

remember a few years ago, just after outlining similar thoughts on a blackboard to a group of students at a summer workshop in the USA, I walked through the ceramics workshop, and on the blackboard was a drawing of an egg, with a flowing lipped flange growing from its top. This re-emphasized my point completely. I would have liked to have met the tutor concerned, as our thinking seemed in parallel, but the opportunity didn't arise as the college was in summer recess. Now that drawing in fact represents the basis of what I call my sun-hat box, which is exactly a combination of this hat image and that egg image, both modified to create the desired design.

It is essential that shapes are correct within the confines of any formulae applied, and on numerous occasions in the past my attention has been drawn to objects where this has not happened. A common

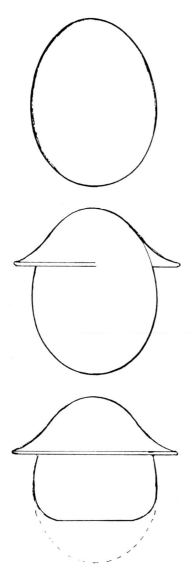

An egg form adapted to create a box

example with which students confront me is their interpretation of a design featured in my last book *Woodturning and Design* (Batsford, 1985) published as *Woodturning: A Designer's Notebook* in the USA: this is what I call a capsule box. Their question is usually that although they have the two-fifths/three-fifths relationship correct, the box does not look right – why? What is wrong is usually very obvious to the trained eye. Instead of continuing straight a little, before being nicely domed, the lid has become more angular and diamond shaped, and so the soft lines required do not exist – this in turn foreshortens the image and destroys the proportion. Another common fault is that the soft curve leading to the base has become a true radius, or that the base diameter is too large, which both result in the form having less life than it should have.

These in particular are the main areas where errors occur which destroy the formulae and proportions of designs you are trying to create, so beware of them.

Design inspiration

The creation and design process takes a lot of thought, and a lot of looking. To develop your skills you will need to embark on a journey down the road of discovery, experimentation, observation, interpretation, exploration, inspiration, and perspiration, all of which will prove to be important elements in the quest. The thoughts and suggestions I offer are all the fruits of my own particular journey thus far, which still continues.

Most designs evolve from a basic shape, which you can manipulate to offer a number of design options all based on the initial idea; and through subtle changes you will be able to develop a theme. Take, for example, a simple straight-sided box with a $\frac{2}{5}$ lid to $\frac{3}{5}$ base proportion. This is about as simple as you can get, yet the basic shape offers tremendous possibilities. For instance, a small 3 mm ($\frac{1}{8}$ in) radius on the lid and base, increasing to 6 mm ($\frac{1}{4}$ in) and to 9 mm ($\frac{3}{8}$ in) will give an increasingly softer look. A series of incised ring lines in the top; a dimple; a button effect; concave lines; convex lines; an applied bead; chatter work – the variations are infinitely variable and all wrought from one basic shape. Many of my designs are based on this principle, and one idea spawns many others.

Selection of capsule boxes. From left to right: Maccassar ebony, spalted beech, birdseye maple. Foreground: *desert ironwood*

Some of the shapes I have developed over the years do not seem to owe anything to my observations, since I created them on the lathe as pleasing tactile aesthetic forms in response to the material or my mood. Many, though, are conscious interpretations of the world around us. Some are obscure until explained, others self-explanatory. Fashion, buildings, nature, street objects, armaments, space, and the sea-shore, all play a part in my design vocabulary. I copy none of them directly, but use them as springboards for development and interpretation.

From the world of fashion, hats have been a recurring inspiration: the bowler, the boater, the sun hat, the coolie, the top-hat, and so on, all form the basis of a theme. These designs are all boxes, but take the elements apart and they become design shapes for bowls. Think of the bowler hat upside-down. Experiment!

Buildings are another rich source of ideas, which as yet I have delved into only slightly, but an interpretative range based on a pagoda has proved very successful. Buildings that dominate cities around the world offer much inspiration, many being the religious buildings from the Far East, Africa, India and the Eastern Block countries: temples, mosques, shrines, palaces, and churches. Even state and governmental buildings offer great potential.

On a less grand level, I gain inspiration from street objects, from humble litter bins to flower tubs, signs, and bollards. The pillar box is a recurring theme in my work.

Space gave me a range of Saturn boxes, as did the space capsules used by USA astronauts. Armaments gave rise to a range of bullet shapes, although they are not obviously recognizable as the source.

Nature probably provides more inspiration to craftspeople and artists than any other, its possibilities as a source are endless. Many woodturners who use nature for their inspiration seem drawn to fruits and nuts particularly, but this can be very limiting, because most people demand and expect that something based on a fruit or nut should look exactly like those to be found in nature, rather than someone's perhaps strange figment of imagination.

Sketches of hats that form the basis of some of my designs: (a) *boater,* (b) *bowler,* (c) *coolie,* (d) *sun,* (e) *topper*

51

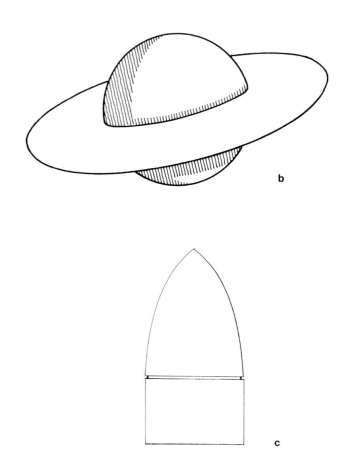

(a) Drawing of a pagoda, the basis of some of my designs (b) The planet Saturn was the inspiration for boxes at one time, where the flange was a different timber from the body (c) A bullet, or church window, whichever interpretation you prefer

What one is being asked to create is a copy, which leaves the craftsman with little room for any personal interpretation, and for this reason this is an area of work I normally avoid. My feeling is that since nature always does things so much better than man, why try to compete?

Having said that, I recognize that from a sales point of view people are drawn to objects that have this strong reflective image drawn from nature. It is a form of comfortable association through easily recognized forms, and there is no doubt that it achieves high sales. But for me, at least, this area represents craftwork without the creative thought process. I allowed myself to enter this field on just one occasion – a joint project for the *New York Times* in the mid eighties for 500 apple boxes, of which I made half. In fact I made 252, two more than needed, so I kept one, and gave the other to my timber supplier. This exercise was enough to make me vow never to enter· this field again, for the feeling of restriction was extremely inhibiting. There are a great many people creating some wonderful fruits and nuts, but this is just not an area for me.

Natural objects do form the basis of a number of my designs, but the casual viewer would find it difficult to identify the source.

All the illustrations in the following chapters are designed to give you ideas; to act as starting points rather than as objects to copy. Truly original designs are very difficult to come up with, because so many options, whatever the object you are making, have been explored over the centuries. But the important thing is for you to develop your own creative potential, and to create what is original for you: and then that spark of creativity and originality will invariably shine through in your work.

Technique

People who become wrapped up in 'designing' can often ignore that element of paramount importance – technique. Often, design and technique are regarded as separate skills, and it is true that a good workman is not necessarily a great designer. But you cannot undertake the creative design process without considering the techniques involved in the making, and equally, your choice of technique will depend on the design requirements of each particular piece, and its ultimate use. Will it be functional or ornamental? Will it be individual or one of a group? Is it designed to surprise, have dramatic impact, or feel comfortable and familiar? How will the technique affect these aims, and how can it best be used to achieve them? These are the sorts of questions you must ask yourself. Never fail to consider the design-technique relationship; they are inextricably linked. Although you will have mastered the basic techniques of woodturning, always be ready to learn more and to use your knowledge to enhance and develop a design. Keeping the practical, functional and aesthetic design requirements in the forefront of your mind as you plan and work each

piece will help you find the best techniques for realising your design. The ability to be flexible in your technical approach will allow you to respond far more sensitively to your material. Exploit the design-technique relationship well, and you will find the whole creative process becomes on-going, and far more satisfying.

Each of the following chapters covers a particular range of objects, and in each I aim to give guidelines, suggestions and starting points for further exploration and discovery. The examples are just that, examples – they are not projects to copy. In each case I touch upon design requirements, materials, proportions, techniques and procedures – all the suggestions are based on my own experience, and none are definitive. My intention is to motivate, to inspire you to explore, to master your own design and technical skills, and so to begin to realize your own potential.

Two hundred and fifty-two apple boxes, made from apple wood for the New York Times

7
Platters and dishes

7
Platters and dishes

The making of platters and dishes provides the face-plate turner (perhaps the term head-stock turner is best used these days, as the advent of the various multi chucks has lessened the use of face plates a great deal) with an area to work in where there can be a total absence of compromise. It is possible to create objects of tremendous visual beauty that can at the same time be totally functional.

First I shall set out a range of proportions that determine the difference between a platter and a dish. The word platter is somewhat archaic; we would call it a plate today. Therefore to make platters, thin discs of wood are called for. Dishes need something a little thicker. A dish to me is something between a platter and a bowl, and it usually has a concave internal shape, whereas the platter is flat.

The intended function of a dish or a platter is usually obvious, and as I have said, this is one case where something can be useful as well as visually beautiful. The question I want to consider in this chapter is – how is the design/technique relationship affected according to whether you are making an individual piece, or producing a batch?

Selection of different platter and dish edge treatments

Proportion

These are some useful guidelines for the thickness and diameters of the material. They will help to keep things in proportion, assuming the wood is not badly distorted and warped.

PLATTER

Thickness	Diameter
19 mm ($\frac{3}{4}$ in)	230 mm (9 in)
25 mm (1 in)	305 mm (12 in)
32 mm ($1\frac{1}{4}$ in)	356 mm (15 in)
38 mm ($1\frac{1}{2}$ in)	457 mm (18 in)
45 mm ($1\frac{3}{4}$ in)	533 mm (21 in)
50 mm (2 in)	686 mm (27 in)

DISH

Thickness	Diameter
25 mm (1 in)	230 mm (9 in)
32 mm ($1\frac{1}{4}$ in)	305 mm (12 in)
38 mm ($1\frac{1}{2}$ in)	356 mm (15 in)
50 mm (2 in)	457 mm (18 in)
64 mm ($2\frac{1}{2}$ in)	533 mm (21 in)
76 mm (3 in)	686 mm (27 in)

The measurements are not categorical – all guides and rules are there to be broken, and you can reach a successful conclusion by disregarding them. But used as a touchstone they should help you create proportionally balanced forms more easily and consistently.

Guidelines for design

The wood must be well seasoned, with less than 10 per cent moisture content if possible.

For highly figured woods, keep the design refined and simple.

For production pieces, where cost is very important, keep designs very simple.

If you are using plain timbers for individual pieces, add detail to give interest.

Quarter sawn boards are the most stable for this type of object, but the figure is usually less interesting, except for those like oak and London plane (sycamore in the USA) in which the rays show tremendous figure when cut in this way.

Highly figured woods are often less stable (apart from quarter sawn) as there is more tension within their growth, and as you cut through the fibres you

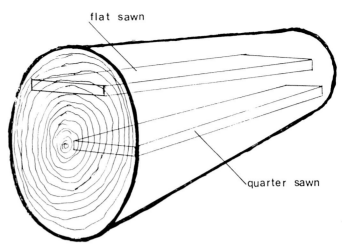

Flat sawn and quarter sawn boards should be cut from a log as shown

release it. You must accept that there will be times when there must be a trade off between stability and visual beauty.

Remember, timber is a living material. Its movements and imperfections often add another dimension to its beauty, but also, on occasions, frustration (it is not like plastic, thank goodness).

The making of any object is best approached through a series of planned step-by-step procedures, be it an individual one-off piece or the production of a number of similar ones (batch production). The approach I am about the describe is the one I use to earn my living.

Design and technique: batch production platters

Batch production work calls for a number of things to be taken into account that are not so critical when it comes to one-offs. You are aiming for fast and quality production, so consider:

For practical designs bases must be large enough for stability, slightly concave to prevent rocking (so avoid glue joint, double-sided tape and vacuum chucking methods for this reason, even though they are often quicker); and should allow access for fingers under the edge to lift the platter from any surface. Simplicity of design, material costs, time, methods and quality are all of importance, particularly if you are aiming to sell what you make on the open market, since you will be entering a very competitive field where there will be a number of efficient makers producing similar objects. To help you achieve some of these aims, you will need to select wood of a modest price, that will work with a minimum of difficulty.

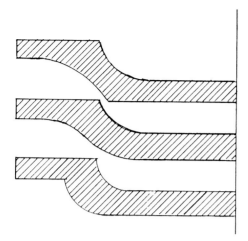

Flange edges that allow the fingers to lift the piece easily

For example, let us say you want to make twenty ash platters. It is best to go for ash that is dry, mild grained, and not badly warped. A standard size might be diameter 305 mm (12 in), thickness 25 mm (1 in). For fast, quality production, these are the technical considerations to bear in mind.

Holding the work on the lathe; face plate, screw chuck, and face plate rings, offer you the best options. Face plates are a slow method, unless you have a lot of them. If you have just one or two, the need to stop to remove and screw them on to another platter disc, constantly breaks the rhythm and speed of your work. The screw chuck represents the fastest and most direct form of holding, the parallel 9 mm (⅜ in) stainless or high speed steel ones offering the best holding properties. With these screw penetration will need to be 12 mm (½ in). The only problem with this method is that if the wood is warped it can rock on the screw (you can shim under the non-seating area but be careful); or, if you have a dig in, it can spin on the screw. My usual method is the screw chuck if the wood is flat and sound, otherwise I use face plate rings. These are low in price when compared to face plates: I have twenty of them in constant use. I secure them to the disc with Robertson hardened headed self-tapping screws, which have a square location depression in the head, and are better than any other screw for securing wood on the lathe, usable time and time again with little wear. Used in conjunction with a magnetic bit held in a power screwdriver, the method is quick: three screws with a penetration of 9 mm (⅜ in) are all that is required. I mount a self-centring four jaw chuck with dovetail jaws (the

quickest acting accurate chuck there is) on the lathe; the face plate rings have a dovetail recess that the jaws locate in. This method represents a very safe and quick way of locating and holding any work of this nature.

When you begin, you should have your design proportions and the piece's required function well fixed in your mind. All your tools for the job should be sharp and at hand allowing you to proceed speedily and efficiently. When you are ready to start shaping the back of your platter, I recommend a Glaser 12 mm (½ in) deep fluted bowl gouge for 95 per cent of the shaping, because it keeps its edge longer than any other tool on the market. It is expensive, but saves a good deal of time and money in the long run. Straight and curved scrapers should be used very lightly to remove any ripples or undulations from the gouge. Use the same tools to create a shallow recess of around 89 mm (3½ in) diameter by 3 mm (⅛ in) deep in the centre of the base to accommodate reverse chucking.

Power sanding is the quickest method of obtaining a good finish. Take care if you use this method not to soften edges that you require crisp. There is a danger of losing detail if you power sand, so if detail is important in your design, you will need to hand sand in the traditional way.

After sanding you will need to apply a liberal coating of oil, my choice being a clear teak oil (a thin liquid paraffin). Then you can sand again in the traditional hand-held way: 240 grit super flex wet and dry paper, will give you an excellent silky satin finish. Once you have applied another coat of oil and buffed dry with soft shavings and cloth, you should have the back of the platter totally finished without tool marks, torn grain, and sanding scratches, and all that has been accomplished so far should not have taken longer than fifteen minutes, including all preparation and mounting on the lathe.

Remove the piece from the lathe, mount the next one, and so on, and shortly you will have all twenty at the same stage. Using the above technique will bring a rhythm, speed and efficiency to your work; it can also bring boredom, which is why I do not like very large quantities.

You can use the same bowl gouge and scrapers for the face of the platter. Scraping should account for no more than 5 per cent of the tool work. Bear in mind that if your piece has a flange it is best created and tool-finished prior to the removal of the centre core. When the centre core is removed, tension may be released and the timber may distort, so if you go back to the edge later, you may well create an edge of inconsistent thickness. Better safe than sorry!

After sanding, oiling and buffing, the total time from wood selection to finished piece should be no more than thirty minutes – twenty-five is the aim. The quality should be high, the design functional and simple.

Design and technique: individual platters

Your considerations here will be slightly different; you will want to choose your timber more for visual effect, and while your design will still take function into account, you will need to highlight features, and pay attention to detail and refinement through subtlety and tactile qualities.

All your preparation methods and tools will remain broadly the same as described previously. However, individual work requires a more flexible and less conceived approach to the design elements, leaving room to respond to the inherent qualities of the material as they are uncovered during the making process. That is not to say you do not have a good idea of what design you are aiming for when you start, but as you proceed a better solution may be thought applicable. To allow for this response you will need to stop the lathe more often to investigate the possibilities, which will of course add time to the making process but will be well worth the patience and exploration. Hopefully, through this approach, you will achieve a far more sympathetic response to the material, and the creation of something of true beauty.

Burr oak platter, brown-hearted and normal oak colour, 500 mm (19¾ in) diameter

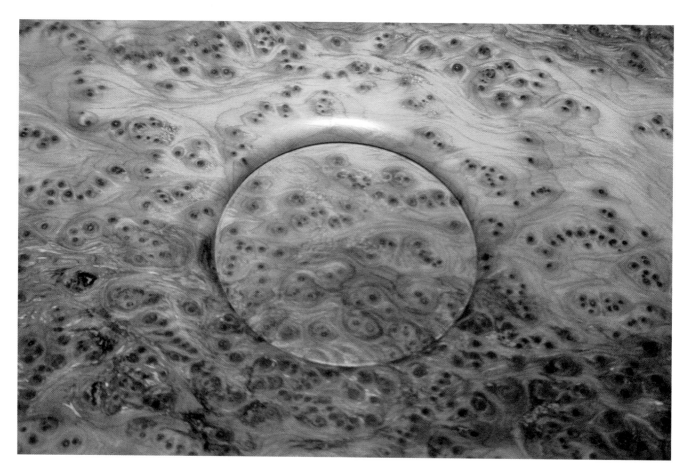

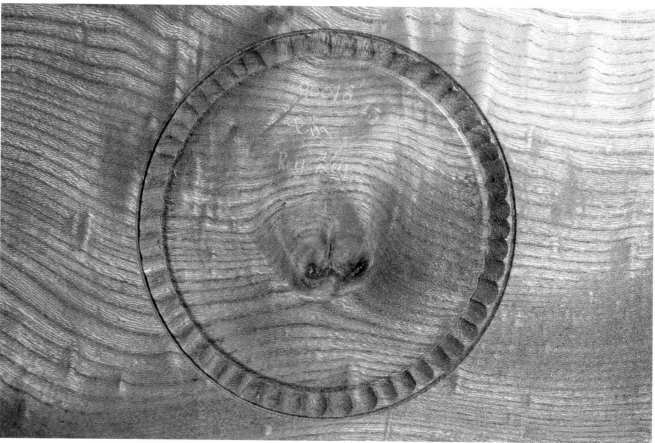

Top left: *Burr yew dish showing the detail in the base, achieved by reverse turning*

Bottom left: *Elm platter, 635 mm (25 in) diameter. The base detail has been carved*

Changes in the actual making process are designed for added refinement: power sanding now goes down to 400 grit, as does hand sanding. Most platters or dishes that exhibit fine figure seldom get used, usually being displayed to show their beauty. The oil finish I use on objects of use is not suitable for visual display objects, as it attracts dust and grime in time, if not used. There are of course oils that contain driers to prevent this happening, but they normally darken the wood, particularly if it is light in colour. So I would choose instead a pre-catalyzed satin cellulose lacquer, which needs twenty-four hours drying time but will not attract dust or affect the wood's colour.

A change in the hand sanding technique is called for here; oil should not be used as a sanding lubricant, since it is not compatible with cellulose. Use a soft white or clear paste wax which is – it does a similar job to the oil.

Any chuck recess in the base will need attention. Almost every piece of individual work I make is reversed for refinement or has some other detailed attention applied to it. As a maker I believe you should take a pride in every part of the piece: poorly finished bases detract from the beauty of the rest, and tell a great deal about the maker's pride in his or her work. With all the chucking methods now available there is no longer any excuse for not finishing the base to the same quality as the rest of the work.

8
Boxes and containers

8
Boxes and containers

I have been producing boxes since 1973 and have by now made many thousands of them, yet making them still gives me a great deal of pleasure. I guess that the need to exercise the precision skills learnt while I was a pattern-maker, coupled with a freedom to create works that are limited only by the imagination, gives me a satisfaction on both counts. Also they are of small scale; they can be made quite quickly from some exquisite materials; and the best are miniature works of art.

Two-tone boxes. From left to right: anjan, (body) ziricote, African blackwood; (lids) birdseye maple, and burr thuya. The largest is 127 mm (5 in) tall

Making the assumption that boxes have a practical function, and are to be used for the storage of rings, pills, coins, powder, or something similar, there is inevitably an overlap between function and design.

Proportion

Balanced designs are created by good proportion, and most of my boxes rely on a range of four ratios which always work. However, the forms developed within these constraints must be correct, or they look totally wrong. The ratios I use are as follows,

being the proportions you see when the box is assembled:

$\frac{2}{3}$ lid : $\frac{1}{3}$ base

$\frac{4}{9}$ lid : $\frac{5}{9}$ base

$\frac{1}{3}$ lid : $\frac{2}{3}$ base

$\frac{2}{5}$ lid : $\frac{3}{5}$ base

The ratio I use most often is two-fifths for the lid: three-fifths for the base. Within these parameters, height, diameter, base size, beads, flanges, and so on must all be of the correct proportion, or the result will be unbalanced, unrefined, heavy, lifeless pieces.

These guidelines and suggestions should help to point you in the right direction and give you a basic understanding of how to work successfully within these confines. The two-thirds lid: one-third base ratio requires that the base has a solid appearance and that the lid is shaped in a way that creates a light, refined image. Otherwise, the base becomes totally dominated by the scale of the lid proportion. The bullet or arched window-style box illustrated on page 52 gives you the clue to achieving this objective: taller, stretched shapes work best.

Selection of boxes in rare burr rippled olivewood 50 mm (2 in) diameter

The four-ninths lid: five-ninths base ratio gives little room for error in the design of the shapes you develop, because it is so near to the almost unworkable equation of equal height for both base and lid, which usually results in the creation of a lifeless form. The bowler hat style and the very squat clam both have the same proportions but are very different in their height and diameter relationship.

The one-third lid: two-thirds base ratio is best served by a box which is taller than its diameter. It is also a formula where the lid being smaller in diameter than the base allows for the creation of many successful designs. One of my most repeated designs, using this ratio, has been a series of shape developments for lids based on a finial style.

The two-fifths lid: three-fifths base ratio offers the most uninhibiting opportunity for balanced design creation. All the suggested areas from which you might seek your inspiration can be translated into workable forms using this proportional ratio.

Guidelines for design

Boxes are best made from end-grained timber for stability. Close-grained, dense hardwoods are best, as dry as possible: less than 10 per cent moisture content is preferable.

They should have well fitting lids, which do not fall off when turned upside down.

The size is important, and best if confined to no larger than 90 mm (3½ in) in diameter for two reasons. First, once timber is used over this size the fit of the lid becomes less predictable, because the wood responds to atmospheric changes by shrinking and swelling slightly. This affects the fit of the lid, and the larger the diameter the more pronounced it becomes.

Secondly, boxes tend to be purchased by ladies, whose hand span does not generally exceed this diameter comfortably. As wood is a wonderfully tactile material it should be handled to give complete satisfaction and pleasure, and a small box, made correctly, affords this experience through the fact that the complete box must be handled to remove the lid.

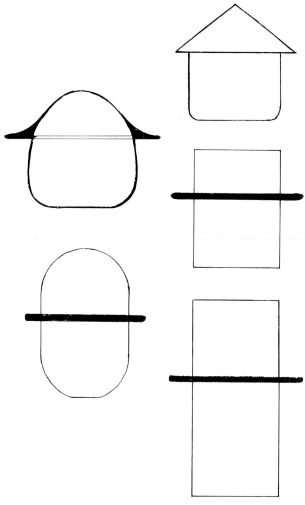

Above: *Clam boxes*. Left to right: *ziricote, burr yew, Honduras rosewood*

Left: *Hat shapes used as the basis for finished boxes*

Loose, ill-fitting lids on boxes up to this size are not acceptable to me – they smack of shoddy workmanship, and a lack of attention to detail. Larger containers, such as powder bowls, are a different matter entirely; they would be impractical if the lid were tight. The size of the object and its use demand that the lid be easily removed without difficulty to gain access to the contents. The materials used will be less stable because of the increase in size – in fact it is usual to use cross-grained timber for these objects. Remember, cross-grained timber is far less stable than end-grain.

The interior of the piece should be of the same quality as the exterior, and the contours of the interior should follow those of the exterior wherever possible. The intention is to ensure that an equal tension is contained within the piece, thereby limiting movement when atmospheric changes take place.

Design and technique

There are many ways of holding the work in the lathe, and many tools you can use. I make all my boxes using a self-centring four jaw chuck and a spigot chuck, because used correctly they are safe and quick; as well as a roughing gouge, a skew chisel, a small spindle gouge, a parting tool and a scraper. I bring variations in shapes and sizes into play according to the size, shape, and density of the timber.

The type of lid fit you intend will decide the holding method, as will the size and shape of the box. There are many lid fitting methods, but I tend to use only three. One is a solid in-fit; the second an in-fitting spigot with the lid hollowed out; the third and most

used has the lid fitting over a spigot. If you want to turn two boxes together, go for cylinders from 32 mm (1¼ in) up to 76 mm (3 in) in diameter, and around 133 mm (5¼ in) in length. For this the boxes will usually need to be of the over-fitting spigot type, the first box made totally in the four jaw chuck, and the second with the interior of its lid made in the four jaw, but the rest made in the spigot chuck. This is safer and saves timber. The length and diameters given are those that work with little trouble, if you are careful, held in a four jaw chuck. Longer lengths of smaller diameter should be chucked in other more positive ways: small and shorter work holds well in the small spigot chuck. Whatever you hold in the lathe, try to distribute the load through chucking methods that give stability, in order to minimize vibration and most other forms of nuisance, while affording safe leverage.

When you come to the making, if you mount your cylinder in your chuck and part off a section for the lid with the narrowest parting tool you have, this will minimize grain mismatch, (mine is less than 2 mm ($\frac{1}{16}$ in)). To allow the grain to match through, remember to invert the lid section when you mount it. When you hollow out, if you use a 9 mm ($\frac{3}{8}$ in) standard spindle gouge with an obtuse 60/65 degree ground angle, you will find that this affords strength and provides the opportunity to rub the bevel through most of the cutting procedure. You could use ring and hook tools, but the dense hardwoods used for these boxes make their use less practical than when used with the temperate woods. All end-grain objects are best hollowed out from the centre, the opposite to the method for cross-grained objects. As with the platters, you should aim to use the gouge for 95 per cent of the work, before moving on to an appropriate scraper for removing any ripples or undulations.

For sanding, narrow folded strips of wet-and-dry paper – 150 grit down to 400 grit – using polish as a lubricant, will minimize friction heat and ring scratches. Take great care not to soften the entrance to the lid as it is this area which will give you the desired friction fit. Use 0000 steel wool for the final finish. A Toluene-based polish will enhance the grain without looking synthetic, which can be the case with lacquers applied on very dense timbers. On the other hand, if you have an open-grained wood, it is fine to seal it with cellulose satin lacquer prior to the final finishing.

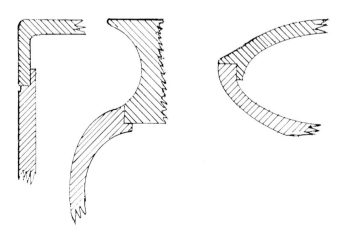

Different styles of lid fittings

Pagoda style boxes. Left to right in five, six and four stacking pieces respectively: *Spalted beech, Indian rosewood, and ziricote*

When you come to creating the exterior form I would recommend spigot lengths from 4 mm–7 mm ($\frac{3}{16}$–$\frac{5}{16}$ in). Anything shorter, and the spigot will wear and become loose in time. With the lid fitted, when you start to create the shape required, bear in mind that a gouge and chisel give cleaner surfaces than a scraper, so it is wise to keep any scraper use to a bare minimum. It is very important to remove the lid and hollow out the base prior to sanding, or the base will shrink and the lid will be loose. You need to keep the functional design requirements of your box and the fit of the lid in the forefront of your mind the whole time.

You will need to take care when parting off and finishing the base: for a stable box, the base must be slightly concave. Parting down to about 6 mm ($\frac{1}{4}$ in) then cutting off with a saw, cutting a spigot on a waste block and inverting the base of the box will allow you to finish this successfully.

A simple box made in the way described should take 30 to 45 minutes to complete. They can be made more quickly of course, but lower standards and less dense woods would be required, or the batch production of simple repetitive designs.

You should still have enough material left for the next box, where the process is almost identical except that the spigot chuck is also brought into use. Using both chucks is a very safe and timber saving method, important if you use expensive and rare woods.

I tend to reserve using the spigot chuck method from the start for the production of the in-fit lidded style of box, where reversing and lid hollowing are not required. There are many, many other ways of chucking, of course, and these are simply my best suggestions; they are the ones I use exclusively. Your own skills and personal designs will undoubtedly dictate the best technique for you – this is simply a starting point. As you develop your technique and design abilities you should feel the need to stretch them through the production of more involved and creative pieces. If you do not, stagnation is likely to set in, so experiment, and never stop looking for the next challenge.

9
Vases and Vessels

9
Vases and Vessels

I have used vases and vessels in the title of this chapter because they seem both to be applied to any enclosed piece of hollow turned work. The dictionary definition of 'vessel' is normally applied to round hollow receptacles which are for domestic use, without reference to any decorative qualities; however, most woodturners seem to apply this term (particularly in the USA) to any enclosed form. Contrary to that dictionary definition, almost all are created to give purely visual pleasure, without thought of use.

The term vase seems more appropriate, given that vases, through definition, are accepted as being truly ornamental. They are usually taller than their diameter, which gives the opportunity to create particularly elegant forms that automatically have an ornamental feeling.

Grass vases or weed pots

You cannot create much simpler purely decorative objects than these. They are usually solid pieces of wood fashioned into pleasing shapes, with a hole drilled in the top, and as such they do not really fit the description of vases and vessels outlined above. But they can be included here because they are decorative and usually have twigs and grasses displayed in them, just as a vase often does. These that I intend to describe are solid, and so are very simple from the making point of view. However they do provide an ideal opportunity to develop simple flowing forms and to improve your turning technique. Small offcuts, mishapen scraps, tree roots, and branches, can all be used – the costs are minimal but the experience can be rich.

The vases illustrated owe their creation to nature, the onion being their inspiration. The smallest is based on a shallot, the next a Spanish onion, and the largest is an elongation of these basic forms.

Onion

The simple nature of these vases is of the essence, and however uncomplicated the design, they should be created to the highest standard in both design and craftsmanship – and the simplest shapes can in some ways be the most challenging.

Proportion

Here are a few sizes that will give you a guide to scale and proportion, but there is a great deal of room for development.

Shallot

Onion grass vases in olive ash

All can be end-grain turned, but of course there are alternatives. Think of the two smallest shallot designs being made in this way, and the larger one from cross-grained material.

Guidelines for Design
Design and technique: end-grain

Your methods will depend very much on whether you are using cross-grain or end-grain (best suited to vases that are taller than their diameter). These suggestions may help.

For the end-grain pieces think of turning cylinders between centres, because this will allow you to obtain three of the smallest and two of the middle size ones from one chuck mounting. You will need of course to allow enough length for chuck waste and parting tool widths between each one. Your holding

SHALLOT

Height	Diameter
45 mm ($1\frac{3}{4}$ in)	64 mm ($2\frac{1}{2}$ in)
58 mm ($2\frac{1}{4}$ in)	89 mm ($3\frac{1}{2}$ in)
76 mm (3 in)	114 mm ($4\frac{1}{2}$ in)

SPANISH ONION

Height	Diameter
89 mm ($3\frac{1}{2}$ in)	70 mm ($2\frac{3}{4}$ in)
108 mm ($4\frac{1}{4}$ in)	96 mm ($3\frac{3}{4}$ in)
127 mm (5 in)	102 mm (4 in)

ELONGATED ONION

Height	Diameter
89 mm ($3\frac{1}{2}$ in)	63 mm ($2\frac{1}{2}$ in)
114 mm ($4\frac{1}{2}$ in)	70 mm ($2\frac{3}{4}$ in)
140 mm ($5\frac{1}{2}$ in)	89 mm ($3\frac{1}{2}$ in)

methods are of personal choice, but contraction chucks gripping a dovetail spigot are my preference for the sizes suggested. Longer lengths will be best held in a cup or collect chucks; you will need to turn a tenon of not less than 25 mm (1 in) in length for this method. You can use other methods, but these are quick and positive.

For safe turning a lathe speed of between 1200 and 1400 rpm will be fine. The aim is to create a simple, flowing form. I would normally use a roughing gouge, skew chisel and parting tool to create the basic shape. It is possible to create shapes of this nature competely using a spindle gouge, a 12 mm (½ in) being ideal, and then a skew or beading tool for blending the curves, which should be soft and fluid. Attention to detail is as always, very important, and to this end I like to see the holes in the tops of such vases nicely softened, not left hard and uncared for. I use a very small gouge or a skew chisel for this, and then all that needs to be done are the sanding and finishing. When it comes to the base

Stretched onion vases

there are several options open to you. The simplest and quickest method is to part off, and disc sand the base flat, apply polish and buff on a calico mop wheel. The most satisfactory, although more time-consuming, method is to part off and reverse into a wooden jam or spigot chuck, thus allowing the base to be totally tooled: this gives the most complete finish. Another option is to mount on a metal mandrel that fits the drill hole, bringing the tailstock up to the base to give support and friction drive. With this method there will be a pip in the middle that needs finishing off either by hand, or with a small disc held in a pillar drill.

These and other methods are all possible; I have refrained in the main from giving specific tool sizes and cylinder lengths, to give you freedom for personal choice. If you decide to make the vases in batches, don't finish them off completely one at a time, leave all the bottoms for one finishing session.

Design and technique: cross-grain

You will achieve a better visual effect from cross-grained timbers on squat forms. Cross-grain is nor-

Hollow rippled white ash vessels. The tallest is 178 mm (7 in) with 4–5 mm ($\frac{3}{16}$ in) wall thickness

mally best for pots whose diameters are larger than their height. The use of cross-grain calls for entirely different procedures from start to finish. Select a piece of suitable timber and treat it just as if you were going to make a small bowl mounted on a screw chuck. The only change is that as well as drilling a small hole for your normal screw chuck, you must drill a larger hole for a plug to be inserted. Once you know the diameter of the hole, turn a cylinder for it in ebony or a similar contrasting wood, parting off a series of short plugs. Once you have turned, sanded and finished the vase remove it from the lathe and what you will have is a pleasant shape which has unfinished bottom containing a large hole. Insert your ebony (or similar) plug, let the glue dry, turn the base, and finish off. The plug makes a nice visual contrast and tells the buyer that the maker takes pride in his work.

All these procedures and methods can be applied to any object of this nature.

Enclosed hollow forms

This area of woodturning has developed principally in the past twenty years or so, originating in the USA but now practised world wide. An industry has developed which produces a whole range of strange and wonderful tools, allowing the average turner to make a reasonable stab at creating something acceptable.

David Ellsworth has been the pioneer and guru, creating an almost cult following through his charismatic personality and creative ability. He has developed unique techniques and tools that allow him to create his works of art. Others, like Mel Lindquist and Ed Moulthrop, have been equally pioneering in their treatments of the vessel form, but the almost totally enclosed eggshell-wall thickness vessel, hollowed out through a very small orifice, is very much an Ellsworth creation. There are now hundreds and possibly thousands of turners throughout the world creating enclosed hollow vessels, but very few ever reach the standard that David sets.

My own work in this field is, I think, about ten years behind David, and it will be a surprise if I ever close the gap, as he is always opening up new frontiers and pushing back the boundaries. Enclosed vessels are his speciality, whereas they form only a small part of my work; however, I do enjoy making them, as they always present a challenge.

You can find a great deal of enjoyment, and much frustration in this sort of work, but you will not create a masterpeice until you have made a good number and had some disasters. A cautious approach is by far the best to start with. Smallish pieces, with a reasonable size hole, are good to begin with. Wet wood that works easily, end-grain turned, is good for practice, and for sorting out the techniques required to create a few basic forms. As your ability and confidence grow, increase the diameters and heights, and make the entrance holes smaller: each will increase the degree of difficulty and provide your next challenge. Much greater concentration and control than usual are called for – there is little time to relax. One false move in the making, particularly as you come near to completion, can destroy many hours of work. Your commitment and ability will be tested to the limit, as the making time becomes longer and more arduous. Turning hollow enclosed forms is not an easy way to make a living. Many buyers seem rather reluctant to pay a truly realistic price for these objects on a regular basis.

Guidelines for design

Vessels or vases have purity of form as their basis. Soft and fluid lines predominate, curves and surfaces are free of flats and undulations, and the forms should be a joy to handle: tactile, balanced, full of life and poise. Any embellishment should be restrained, used to frame an opening or highlight a change of surface direction. I trust that the photographs reflect these obejctives.

These are a number of ideas that may help you develop themes, or stimulate the thought process when you select your material.

Just as the onion form was the basis for my grass vase shapes, I have used here the popular image of a heart, and the unusual image of a hot-air balloon profile. The most unlikely subjects can spur the imagination into working creatively!

Vessels. From left to right: *burr brown oak* (*hot-air balloon profile*), *spalted beech* (*heart shape profile*)

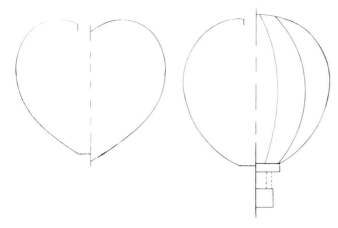

Hot-air balloon and heart shapes, showing how they are modified and used in the creation of hollow vessels

By far the most common approach is to make the whole vessel smooth, removing all the spiky growth areas. If you keep the top surface as large as possible, before the soft curves start, this will allow you to exploit the budd-eye feature to the maximum. This principle can also be applied to those woods that display strong contrasting sapwood to heartwood growth characteristics, although the turning of hollow vessels in this way is more difficult, as they will be made from cross-grain material. The outside is no problem, but hollowing cross-grain timber through a small hole is not easy, compared with end grain hollowing.

N.B. The convoluted growth patterns found in burrs result in them working like end-grain. Although the illustration would suggest otherwise, this of course would be so in a normal tree's growth.

The budd-eye effect to be found in burr growth is for me served best by objects that are either squat, or tall and elegant. Which you create will be dictated by how the burr is cut from the log. Squat forms should have the budd-eye growth in the top and be displayed for the viewer to look down on. Tall forms, with the budd-eye growth on the side, should be displayed at a higher level to allow their form and the grain formation to be fully appreciated.

By using similar materials but handling them in a number of different ways it is possible to create effects of marked contrast: this is where the imagination is called upon again. Take a burr, for instance. By removing the bark you should expose a very spiky surface of stunted budd-eye growth. I will suggest just three treatments to you for making the most of this feature, but there are plenty of others. Try using this budd-eye feature at the top of the vessel. The simplest and most direct method is to let the spiky burr remain in its natural state: this will provide a rugged top, while the rest of the vessel is turned smooth and polished. This will create a vessel that is both rugged and formal.

Another, and very effective, approach is to turn the whole vessel smooth except for the area around the aperture, leaving this surrounded by the natural spiky growth.

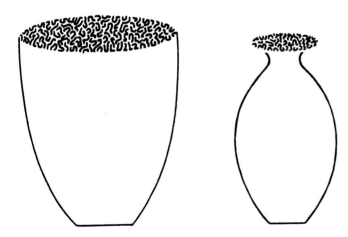

Left: Vessel with full spiky burr top. Right: Vase-shaped vessel with a spiky flange burr top

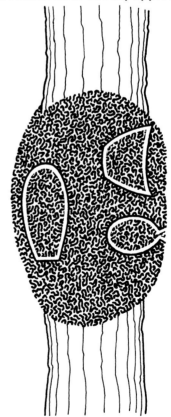

Burr trunk, illustrating where to cut vessels

Heart-shaped burr elm vessel. Note how the void in the side is heart-shaped also. 280 × 178 mm (11 × 7 in)

Design and technique

As I indicated earlier, the making of hollow enclosed vessels demands a number of techniques and tools different from those normally associated with conventional woodturning. Since the techniques involved are complex, I will be a little more specific about procedures than in previous sections.

The early stages of developing a hollow form are normally conventional – turning reasonably true to a cylinder between centres, if the vessel is tall and made from end-grain; and face-plate mounting if it is squat and cross-grained.

To make these objects, mounting on the lathe must be secure and solid. I happily make end-grained vessels up to 254 mm (10 in) in height and 152 mm (6 in) in diameter using the four-jaw contracting

dovetail chuck, which will grip a 64 mm (2½ in) diameter spigot some 6 mm (¼ in) in length. If your timber is sound and your tool skills good, this method of gripping will work well.

For work over these sizes I suggest you secure all end-grain pieces on face plates of suitable size, with a number of screws of good length. This means you will waste the timber where the work is secured, so remember to allow for that when planning your project. As the pieces get larger increase the face-plate size and the screw lengths.

I make cross-grained pieces up to 305 mm (12 in) in diameter and 203 mm (8 in) in height on glued waste blocks, which in turn are secured to a face-plate. For work over this size my normal practice is to screw directly to the block.

Variable-speed lathes are ideal for this sort of work, although I do not have one. My advice would be always to err on the side of caution – use slower speeds rather than faster. The pieces illustrated were nearly all turned at a spindle speed of around 800rpm. Most of the end-grained pieces are 153 mm (6 in) in diameter and 153 mm–228 mm (6 in–9 in) in height. The cross-grained pieces are 254 mm–305 mm (10 in–12 in) in diameter and 102 mm–178 mm (4 in–7 in) in height. Harder and unbalanced timbers would need to be turned at a slower speed. A general rule of thumb is that soft and wet timbers can be cut at higher speeds with larger tools, as there is less cutting resistance; hard woods and imbalanced pieces should be cut at slower speeds with strong tools, which are often a little smaller to lessen the much greater cutting resistance.

Bearing all that in mind, select a lathe speed suitable for the size of work being undertaken, mount your work in the chosen way, and proceed to shape the top two thirds or so of the outside form. Leave the bottom third for final shaping at a later stage; at the moment it will give the solid stability required for the removal of the interior. The making process up to this point has been totally conventional, but from now on it is a different story.

I use the following method for end-grain hollowing. For vessels up to 254 mm (10 in) in height, the first thing required is a hole down the middle, which can be made with a drill, gouge or boring bar, (I usually use a long and strong spindle gouge ground with a short angle, which works like a shell auger, used correctly). If you make the aperture hole around 38 mm (1½ in) in diameter, life should not be too difficult – a considerable amount of material can be removed using the gouge (see page 67). The use of hook and ring tools will allow the removal of even more material prior to changing to the special scraping tools required.

You will need to remove the piece from the lathe on its chuck at very regular intervals throughout the making, to empty the shavings and chaff from within. Remember, do not take too much material out of the lower section of the vessel at this time: you need this to give stability and strength while you gradually thin the wall sections down from the top. This extra material is important as it helps to absorb vibration.

Through a hole of this size a cranked scraper will allow you to do most of the refining of the interior shape. The one problem with this method is that you have to grip the tool very firmly to counteract the torquing on the cutting edge, as this is out of line with the shaft, and will constantly try to twist down and out of your grasp. To counteract this, tools have been developed with bent hooked shafts, which allow the cutting edge to be in line with the shaft, to alleviate the torquing. But these have a problem in turn – the tools have a fixed tip on the hooked crank, which unfortunately to a large degree dictates the form of the object. Others have an Allen-keyed moveable tip on a straight or cranked bar which can be moved to cut in the best position, but with this method you still have the torque problem to a degree. The best and the most widely used tools for creating larger vessels are those that have an adjustable tip in a straight round bar. This cutting tip can be advanced in length and pivoted in many directions. The tool tip passes through a suitably machined hole in a bolt, which in turn passes through a machined slot in the end of the bar, and the whole thing is locked down solid with a nut on the bolt.

Back to the making. You should be working progressively from the top, aiming to create as constant a wall thickness as possible. The thickness is your own choice: much will depend on your ability level. Remember, the thinner you go the greater the skills required, and the greater the risk. If your work is to grow, you need to push yourself; you will blow a few up along the way, but in time you will create much better pieces. I usually aim for a wall thickness of between 3 mm-6 mm (⅛ in–¼ in), depending on the size of the vessel.

Through a hole the size I have described, it is possible to sand the inside to a fair degree. Do so wherever you can reach, but be *extremely* careful – you could break your fingers. Smaller-holed vessels' interiors are usually left straight from the tool.

For the exterior, I normally sand the top two-thirds of the body, already created, and then complete tooling the bottom third. Afterwards I complete the final sanding and finishing however I choose. All that remains is for the piece to be parted off from the waste section and the bottom finished off. This can be done in many different ways, but all have to be carried out with care. Methods such as reversing into hollow chucks, or gripping the body against a wooden faceplate a hollow outer ring tightened down with bolts give complete access to finish off the bottom. These methods take time and contain a higher risk element, but they do allow for the best finishing. A simpler method is to part off and sand,

making the bottom slightly concave with an abrasive pad in the pillar drill.

The procedures for making cross-grained vessels with a much larger aperture are similar to those already described. The main changes of approach are in the internal hollowing and finishing. A bowl gouge can be used to remove a great deal of the interior prior to the use of the scraping tools. As the aperture access is reasonably large, the interior can be finished to the same standard as the exterior.

All this is just a taste of what can be achieved with vases and vessels, designed to fire your imagination and trigger your enthusiasm to tackle such difficult but immensely rewarding pieces.

Top left: *Olive ash cross-grained hollow vessel, 280 × 140 mm (11 × 5½ in) high*

Bottom left: *Detail showing bead round the entrance of the vessel in above photo*

10
Bowls

10
Bowls

Bowls are probably the headstock face-plate turner's most commonly produced item of work. There must be tens of thousands of them produced worldwide every year, but they still hold a tremendous fascination for us all. Perhaps this is because they give the woodturner an opportunity to create objects which have more possibilities for self expression than any other. They can be large, small, thin, thick, deep, shallow, light, heavy, elegant, chunky, bold, restrained, practical, decorative – the list is endless.

In its simplest form a bowl is a piece of wood with a depression in it, a receptacle. However, it has become much more than this. The majority of bowls are still made with function as their primary aim, but many are made purely with the thought of giving visual pleasure. Mark Lindquist summed this up nicely some years ago when referring to one of this bowls. 'It is full already', he said. He was talking about the inherent beauty discovered within the material, and enhanced and communicated through the form created. Those were the words of an artist, and they give another clue as to why the bowl remains a constant challenge to the woodturner, whether artist or production maker.

The subtlety of the curved form presents a constant challenge for the finest makers. The quest for shapes that have some special magic, as David Pye describes them, 'pieces that sing'*, is the driving force for many of us.

The failure or success of this quest lies in the almost intangible subtlety of a curve, the lift of a foot, the flow of a lip – all are elements that may be applied collectively or separately to any bowl form, and when they are right, a perfectly balanced bowl with poise, life and flair emerges, the ultimate reward.

Having achieved this once, you might think it would be achieveable time after time, but this is not so. These elements will prove just as elusive in the next bowl. Creative spontaneity is the secret of success, and you will never capture that if you try to make an exact copy, try as you might: I have said before that a copy seldom has the life and spark of an original. You may ask why, if you have faithfully copied the object. Often it is down to the material. No two pieces of wood are ever the same – similar, yes, but never the same. This is probably the clue to the missing 'spark' in the copy: any slight change in the material's structure probably demanded a response from the maker – it may have called for a very slight change to a curve to reflect this. We are back to spontaneity, that unmeasurable, undefinable quality that makes constant success so elusive. We will make good bowls often; special ones only rarely.

Proportion

	Height	Diameter	Wall thickness
SUGAR BOWL	50 mm (2 in)	102 mm (4 in)	5mm ($\frac{3}{16}$ in)
SIDE SALAD BOWL	102 mm (4 in)	152 mm (6 in)	6 mm ($\frac{1}{4}$ in)
SALAD BOWL	102 mm (4 in)	254 mm (10 in)	12 mm ($\frac{1}{2}$ in)
	102 mm (4 in)	355 mm (14 in)	16 mm ($\frac{5}{8}$ in)
	102 mm (4 in)	405 mm (16 in)	17 mm ($\frac{11}{16}$ in)
	152 mm (6 in)	254 mm (10 in)	12 mm ($\frac{1}{2}$ in)
	152 mm (6 in)	355 mm (14 in)	17 mm ($\frac{11}{16}$ in)
	152 mm (6 in)	405 mm (16 in)	17 mm ($\frac{11}{16}$ in)

These are the ratios I usually apply to domestic bowls. The wall thickness is decreased by 3 mm/4 mm ($\frac{1}{8}/\frac{3}{16}$ in) through the arc of the internal curve from the rim to the base in the larger bowls; this helps to keep the weight down and to retain balance when in use. The thickness of the base normally remains the same as the rim. Again, these are simply basic guidelines: all rules are there to be broken, and all the suggestions are intended as starting points in the search for your personal woodturning identity.

*David Pye, *The Nature and Art of Woodmanship*, Cambridge University Press, 1968.

Guidelines for design

What follows are my thoughts about the design processes for a number of bowl forms from the domestic to the purely visual, and some of the ideas that spark their shapes.

Functional bowls

The starting point has to be that the bowl must fulfil all its basic use requirements: that the contents envisaged will be successfully contained, and that when used it will give much pleasure. If the bowl is to hold granules, for instance, it is best served by being in-curved or at least straight-sided. It should be stable when placed on the table, not easily tipped. These observations automatically lead to certain design constraints. Base sizes must provide for stability, and are best if they are between two-fifths and two-thirds of the overall diameter. I apply this formula to the majority of my functional bowls,

Typical selection of ash and elm salad bowls

since it leaves enough freedom for the creation of shapes that are both pleasing to the eye and stable in use.

Smaller bases can be created and the bowl still remain stable, but the shape of the form becomes much more critical if the balance and stability are to be maintained. I make many salad bowls with a foot size of around a quarter of the overall diameter, but the form has to be right or it becomes unstable. It is no good creating a bowl with a full-bellied curve near the base, if the foot is no more than a quarter of the overall diameter: the whole thing looks, and is, unbalanced. But make the shape open and flared with the same size foot and it works perfectly. This shape acts like a funnel, and when in use the bowl remains balanced and stable as the contents are removed.

Functional bowls need to have strength but at the same time must not be too heavy. They must feel right when lifted – there is no doubt we all have a built-in expectancy of what the weight of a piece will

be when we go to lift it. Many woodturners have a tendency to make rims too thin and bottoms too thick and heavy. Both factors take away a great deal of the pleasure the bowl should provide when handled, because they give an instant feeling of unbalance. Always remember that objects for use should not only fulfil their function but look good and feel right.

Individual bowls

Here you can give free rein to the thought and making process. The possibilities are infinite. However, for our purposes it will be best if we identify a range of shapes to concentrate the mind, and deal with them one at a time. In each section think of the bowl giving visual pleasure rather than being functional, although of course, most could be used.

Shapes are limitless but there are a number of basic starting points – bowls without a foot; bowls with a foot; bowls with flanges (with feet and without); bowls with natural tops or natural bases; bowls that have detail; bowls that do not; and so on. Once you have developed a range of shapes it is possible to treat them in many different ways and achieve results that can be dramatically different, if you are prepared to open your mind and be receptive to the world around you.

Non-footed bowls

These are probably the commonest type of bowl made by the woodturner. I still start with what I consider to be the simplest and easiest bowl that can be made on a lathe. This is open and flared, and little manipulative tool skill is required, as once the cutting starts the action is very repetitive. However, if the result is to be visually successful, you must take into account various design considerations. The size of the base that works best for this type of bowl is normally a fifth to a quarter of the size of the overall diameter. Within these parameters you can create your shapes. To take three examples – one may give a straight image, one may be convex, and one may be concave. The straight image will actually need a slight convex curve to be visually acceptable, otherwise it will look like a concave mistake, with no tautness to the form. A 3 mm–4 mm ($\frac{1}{8}$ in–$\frac{3}{16}$ in) swelling will provide a subtle curve on a bowl of 220 mm ($8\frac{5}{8}$ in) diameter, 102 mm (4 in) high, with a base size of one fifth of the overall diameter. This will give you your desired straight, flared image.

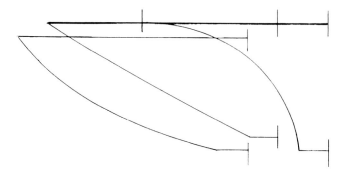

Simple shaped non-footed bowls

To create the convex image on a similar sized bowl a greater swelling of the curve will be called for – how great is a matter for your own judgement.

For the concave image to work successfully you will need to create a much more dramatic curve than that required for the convexed one. As the convex and concave curves increase, your manipulative skills will also need to increase, as will your ability to judge what constitutes a pleasing visual image.

The next form on which to focus is that which I call the globe shape. This, for me, is one of the most satisfying shapes there is – soft and rounded, very tactile, pleasing to look at, but deceptively difficult to get right. There is much pleasure in creating one successfully. The subtlety of the continuous curve which needs to be softened and tightened just in the right places presents a constant challenge. Most of the globe-shape bowls you make will be acceptable, but those that 'sing' and are special will be rare.

The bowls in the photographs demonstrate my point. The small walnut one 'sings', the ash one is poor, and the lime one acceptable. Let us take a look at why I make those judgements. Ultimately it is all about proportion and the curve within the parameters.

The bases of the walnut and lime bowls are just over a quarter of the size of the overall diameter. The outside diameter, at the top of the incurved form, is between 20 mm/25 mm ($\frac{13}{16}$/1 in) smaller than the maximum diameter. In contrast the ash bowl has a base of less than a quarter of the size of the overall diameter, while the outside diameter at the top of the in-curved form is 35 mm ($1\frac{3}{8}$ in) smaller than the maximum diameter. This gives the clue as to why the ash bowl hasn't worked. Although it would have been quite possible to create a pleasing bowl, even with these parameter changes, I simply got it wrong.

Group of globe bowls. From left to right: *burr lime, rippled ash, walnut. The lime bowl is okay but rather ordinary; the ash bowl is poor, having a pointed bottom section; the walnut bowl is just right – and 'sings'*

The curve in the lower section is far too straight resulting in what looks like a pointed lower section, instead of the soft rounded look I was aiming for. The mistake made in the ash bowl is easily recognized, but the lime one needs a little more thought. When put next to the walnut bowl, the reason for its lack of special magic becomes apparent. The curves are not quite tensioned enough: they are a fraction too full, and the piece just does not possess that extra life. It is a near miss.

You will need to keep looking and comparing each bowl you make in this way, trying to recognize what makes the difference between those that are special, good, indifferent, poor, and downright bad. This is how you will learn and develop your designs and techniques. It may also suggest improvements. For instance, I was pleased with the large Claro walnut bowl in its pure turned state, but the fluted carving round the top was what gave it that extra dimension.

Footed bowls

These provide the opportunity to create some of the most elegant and pleasing forms possible, but also the opportunity to produce some of the biggest disasters. The ratio of the height to the diameter of the foot now becomes critical: it must be in proportion, always reflecting the demands of the curves created in the main form of the bowl. Your eye and judgement will be put to the test in the creation of these bowls more than in any other.

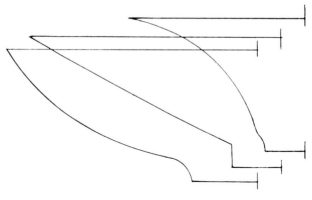

Simple shaped footed bowls

87

Burr claro walnut bowl with carved rim. A favourite.
280 × 178 mm (11 × 7 in)

The flared bowls described above work very well with a foot added. The open, straight flared burr elm bowl has quite a tall foot which is only a fifth of the overall diameter. The open flared ash bowl with more curve has a foot of similar height, but the diameter is increased to almost a quarter of the overall size, to compensate for the increased curve. The concave curve needs a much shorter foot to keep it balanced; this is best between a fifth and a quarter of the overall diameter.

The globe form described in the non-footed bowl section is not served well at all by trying to add a foot. Full curved forms can be made to work, but it is best if the top is not in-curved. Those shown here have quite tall feet with diameters equal to a quarter of the overall diameter. If you look closely at their form you will see that the curve lifts quickly from the foot. In bowls where the curve is kept lower, the base size will need to be increased to around a third of the diameter, and the foot is best kept short or it will look proportionally unacceptable.

As yet I have not made any mention of objects that have inspired my designs: this is because it is virtually impossible to come up with a bowl form that has not been produced at some time. All tend to be refinements, derivatives of those that have already been produced over the centuries. Man is for ever re-inventing the wheel. The one series of bowls that was inspired by observation is the group of bell-like bowls illustrated here. This is most

Top right: *Olive ash and burr elm footed bowls. The ash bowl has a foot size a quarter of the total diameter; the size of the elm foot is a fifth of the total diameter*

Bottom right: *Group of footed full bodied curved bowls. From left to right: burr lime; burr tuliptree; burr oak; largest 190 × 140 mm (7½ × 5½ in) high*

A group of burr elm bowls with different rolled edge treatments, all about 178 mm (7 in) diameter

apparent when they are turned upside-down. All are footed and have base sizes from between a quarter and a fifth of their overall diameter.

Flanged bowls

These can be footed or unfooted. The designs which work on the flanges of platters transfer well to bowls, providing even more scope, as there is more depth available. The proportions outlined in the sections above apply equally to these bowls.

As I have said all along, it is possible to take one basic form and use it to develop a full range of shapes by making fairly simple adjustments. The flange bowls featured here give you ideas for outside profile changes and edge treatments. I usually like to make them with a foot, and with the flange projecting from the main body of the bowl, both features can be linked to the body in various ways. The foot can be straight, dovetailed, or flared; the transition from foot to bowl can be hard — even accentuated with an incised line — through a small

Top left: *Three small bell-shaped burr oak bowls*

Bottom left: *Group of small flange bowls. From left to right: Mexican rosewood (bocote), burr elm, Arabia rajardo, 152 mm (6 in) diameter*

radius, or a smooth, fluid curve. The flange can be similarly linked through the same range of ideas, the smooth, fluid linking curve developing into an ogee, one of the most subtle and rewarding of curves. The top flange profiles offer many choices, and most will work with any of the outside profiles suggested.

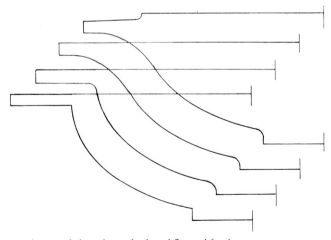

A selection of shape forms for footed flanged bowls

Rolled-edge bowls

Those illustrated show three types. One has the edge rolled externally, one internally, and the other is a combination of both, giving almost the impression of an applied bead. They are extremely tactile pieces, and potters in particular are always drawn to them.

Combination curves

These are very difficult to get right, and any change of direction needs to be positive. The most commonly used combination is the transition from convex curve to concave, with an incised line highlighting the change. They are tricky because you always turn bowls in the vertical plain, but these are always viewed in the horizontal. This sometimes results in a piece that you were happy with on the lathe, being not nearly as successful as you thought when viewed in its horizontal plane. The best solution is to remove the bowl from the lathe periodically (still on its chuck) and set it down on a table. This will give you a chance to see what adjustments you need to make to get it right. To look at it properly, make yourself a box with a hole in the top big enough for the chuck body to pass through, with the base of the bowl level with the top of the box. If you simply set the bowl down on the chuck, the chuck acts as a plinth, giving a very false impression of the bowl.

A *group of small natural topped bowls.* From left to right: *burr lime, yew, burr boxwood. They all took their inspiration from cupped hands with fingers reaching upwards*

Shaped topped bowls

These bowls can range from the extremely graceful to the extremely rugged. Most are natural-topped, ie, the outside of the tree is used to form the top of the bowl. Those that have dramatically contrasting sapwood to heartwood, or a distinctive bark feature, or the spiky outcrop of a burr, are the most dramatic. This sort of bowl first appeared in Britain in the late 1970s, mostly through the development of the very thin wet-turned bowl. Woodturners in the USA were making them long before that – Bob Stocksdale for instance, and Rude Osolnik in particular. The shaped topped bowl must now rate as one of the most exploited bowl forms made. Almost everyone who takes up woodturning as a hobby likes to try his or her hand at making one at least once. Most people select material that is very evenly balanced, in which the two high points and two low points are equal, which results in a very predictable sameness in all these bowls.

Only those who are prepared to take more risks or who have developed their skills to the pitch which allows them to create a style which is instantly recognized as their own are lifted above the crowd.

These makers have developed their talents and skills through heightened awareness and perception.

I deliberately headed this section 'Shaped topped bowls' and not 'Natural topped', for the reason that many of my bowls are shaped after turning, and are not reliant on what nature provides for the top. The shaping that takes place is my conscious decision to

Footed shaped topped bowls after turning. From left to right: *cocobolo, putumuju, lignum vitae*

obtain a particular required effect. I use a pneumatic drum sander for the shaping, and soften the edges by hand sanding and polishing afterwards.

This chapter has hardly scratched the surface of the opportunities and potential for developing your skills in bowl creation, and for once I have said little about the techniques and making processes because there are so many options open when covering such a range of bowls. As ever, design and technique are inter-related, and one should inform the other at every stage. As a general rule, I would expect that most of these bowls would be reverse-chucked and the bottoms finished with a small gouge and scraper. I would think it possible that all the bowl forms suggested could be 90/95 per cent created with bowl gouges, with the use of other tools limited to 5/10 per cent. All normal holding methods will apply.

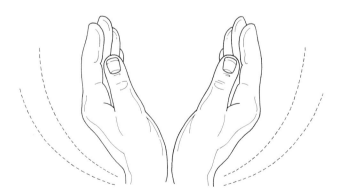

Hands reflecting bowl images, the dotted lines representing more open spaces

11
Sapwood and burrs

11
Sapwood and burrs

Throughout the book the odd photograph or line drawing has shown these features utilized to good effect, but without examining their full potential. It seems appropriate to conclude with a more in-depth look at sapwood and burrs, and to suggest visually how to make the best use of these features.

Sapwood

Sapwood is usually lighter in colour and softer in structure than heartwood. In many of the lighter timbers it is almost indistinguishable from the heartwood, particularly in temperate woods. When temperate hardwoods are used in buildings as structural material, or for furniture and cabinet making, it is usual for most sapwoods to be removed. This is

done for several reasons: sapwood does not have the strength of heartwood; it is susceptible to woodworm attack; and most sapwood is rather murky, lacking the richness of colour and surface quality found in the heartwood. There are exceptions to every rule, of course, and there are sapwoods that do have a dramatic colour contrast, and also a similar density. It is these which offer the woodturner something to exploit.

More exotic timbers than temperate exhibit this characteristic. This is due to their growth cycle. The sapwood in these timbers is often harder than that

Boxes with sapwood and heartwood highlights. From left to right: laburnum, African blackwood (both with sapwood) and Nicaraguan lignum vitae (in this case the heartwood is the highlight)

in the heartwood of many of the temperate timbers. The most dramatic of all contrasts must be that found in African blackwood, whose clean white/ cream sap contrasts strikingly with the black heart. African ebony, although the blackest wood of all, has a very dirty murky sapwood which adds nothing if used. Of the northern temperate timbers, laburnum and yew probably offer the greatest contrast.

Boxes

The photographs here give an insight into the many different ways of making use of sapwood: you will note the tremendous difference between the boxes. One group shows what I am looking for – these have just enough sapwood showing to give the work a highlight – but those in the other group are over-powered by the sap's featureless characteristic.

The boxes with the highlight were cut from small logs, whereas those with too much sapwood show-ing came from bought-in squares. The two different effects resulted from two different techniques: the ones from the log were marked out on the log to include just the right amount of sapwood, while

How to mark out and cut the timber to obtain the best effect using sapwood

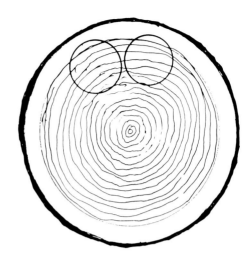

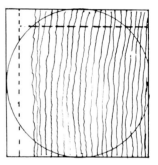

Below: *Boxes where the sapwood is far too dominant*

97

those from the squares utilized all the timber as it came. For a better effect, the squares should have been cut smaller. Cutting a piece from the sapwood side would have reduced its dominance. These boxes are 75 mm (3 in) in diameter, and if they had been reduced in size to 63 mm (2½ in) the desired effect would have been possible. My reason for not doing this in the first place was my desire not to waste wood, particularly if it is an exotic, but by failing to do so I created a piece of work less appealing than it might have been. The lesson to learn is, bigger is not always better. Reduction of the sap would have created a smaller but more desirable and balanced article.

Bowls

The bowls tell their own story in a way, but are worth commenting on. In the *lignum vitae* bowl the sapwood is equally balanced on either side of the rim, while the rest is the heartwood, and the base of the bowl from near the outside of the tree. This is Nicaraguan

lignum vitae, which is much more difficult to turn than the more common West Indian variety. The sapwood is cream, and very clean, giving distinct contrast. The West Indian variety is not so distinct and has a dirty look.

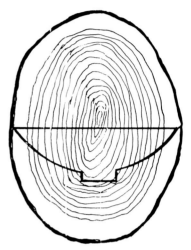

Above: *How the bowl shown below was cut from the log*

Below: *Nicaraguan lignum vitae bowl displaying the clean sapwood*

The African blackwood dish has the sapwood at its base, and it has been turned in a way which allows for part of this feature to be exposed on the inside, giving the effect of a white pool.

The next African blackwood bowl (one of my favourite bowls, made in 1985) has a natural top showing the distinct and highly dramatic contrast of the sapwood to heartwood. It is 216 mm (8½ in) in diameter and 178 mm (7 in) high. The wall thickness is around 3/5 mm ($\frac{1}{8}$/$\frac{3}{16}$ in) throughout. This was quite a difficult bowl to make as the density of the timber and the deep irregular fluting meant I had to turn it at a slower speed than I would have preferred.

African blackwood natural topped bowl, a favourite. 216 × 178 mm (8½ × 7 in)

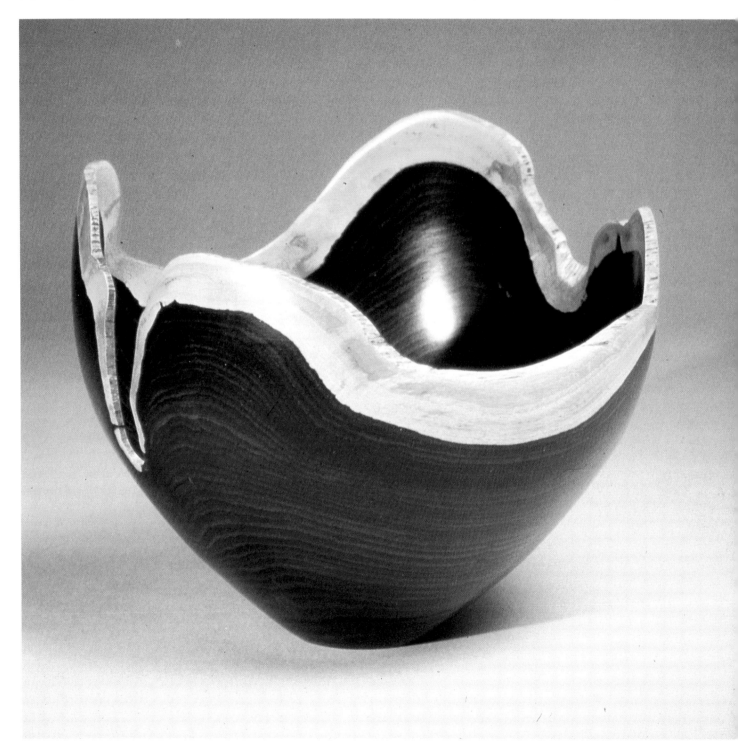

Showing how the bowls in the bottom left photo were cut from the log

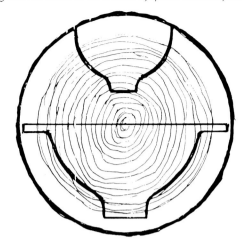

The small group of Mexican rosewood (bocote) pieces shows the two bowls with the sapwood used to good effect. The one with the natural top is self-explanatory; the other, which has sapwood on the foot and the rim of the bowl, is a little more unusual. The top of the bowl is near the heart of the log and the foot to the outside, as the drawing shows.

Top left: *African blackwood dish with sapwood in the base, 203 mm (8 in) diameter.* Bottom left: *Group of Mexican rosewood (bocote) pieces, the largest being 152 × 102 mm (6 × 4 in)*

Burrs

Burrs (burls USA) hold tremendous fascination for all who use wood, and particularly those who turn it. The rich diversity of their structure and the potential they offer are immense. It is very difficult at times not to be beguiled by the incredible beauty that burrs offer, but far too many turners are seduced into feeling that just by exposing and polishing a surface they have created a masterpiece. Expose it, by all means, but surely each maker has a duty to respond to the beauty by creating forms which are strong in their own right, and at the same time a reflection of that inherent beauty. I make these comments because I detect a worrying trend developing. There are far too many beautiful pieces of wood being offered up for sale, rather than wonderful objects being made from beautiful pieces of wood.

Throughout the book there have been photographs of items made from burrs, and these have been mainly formal and precise in shape. This final section is intended to give an insight into ways which

Underside of burr oak flanged bowl pictured on page 105 (top)

will allow for that formality to be combined with the burr's rugged and dramatic characteristics.

Natural topped bowls made from burrs are perhaps the most dramatic you can produce. The 'U'-shaped form has been a recurring theme throughout my work since the mid 1970s. The early pieces were small and totally formal, sometimes with a sapwood splash effect up one side. As my turning has developed the size and depth of pieces have increased, as has the search for increasingly dramatic effects.

This burr oak 'U'-shaped vessel is one of a developing series. It is by no means the largest or most difficult piece I have made, but it is typical.

Small diameter straight-sided works which have depth are far more difficult to make than larger diameter pieces which are deeper, because of the smaller entrance access. Let me illustrate what I mean. The vessel featured here is 305 mm (12 in) high by 203 mm (8 in) diameter, but a similar 381 mm (15 in) high by 305 mm (12 in) diameter vessel was

far easier to make than this one. The simplest vessels of this sort are those with fairly even tops. Those that have a large drop from one edge to the other are more difficult, but are a great deal more interesting. This one has a drop of 102 mm (4 in).

Another natural topped burr oak piece is featured here. This bowl has a very dramatic top. It is 228 mm (9 in) high by 228 mm (9 in) diameter, and there is again a dramatic drop in height from one side to the other. It also has a sculptured look with much lighter coloured sapwood. In this piece, the light colour has been caused by decay – this part of the log had been stored on the ground, and oak sapwood soon rots in this situation. The lower areas are those areas which

Far left: Burr oak 'U'-shaped vessel with natural top, 280 × 203 mm (11 × 8 in)

Below: A dramatic burr oak natural topped bowl, 228 × 228 mm (9 × 9 in)

were too weak to save, so they have been carved away. The light-colour sapwood almost went the same way, but was impregnated and preserved with cyano-acrylic glue (Thin Hot Stuff). This glue has made many things possible for turners today that were impossible before; here the impregnated light sapwood became as solid as the heartwood, and the colour contrast helped give the bowl its dramatic appearance.

Another natural topped bowl is made from burr mulberry. This is one of the easiest woods to turn, and when first made is very dramatic in appearance. However the bright yellow look soon tones down to a dull brown. This is why my plea for strong form comes in. Reliance on the burr's beauty is a mistake, because it is short-lived in timbers like this. It must be remembered that all woods mellow or fade in time; it is the shape that remains. This bowl, made in the early to mid 1980s, is 305 mm (12 in) in diameter, 178 mm (7 in) at its highest point and 102 mm (4 in) at its lowest. The shape, with its burr-like fingers reaching upward and about to roll over at the back of the bowl, has always reminded me of a wave about to break, or of a sea-shell. Whatever, there is at least a very sea-linked image.

The next burr oak bowl is almost totally formal except for the natural spiky burr points, which have been allowed to become part of the wide flanged edge on one side. This bowl is 368 mm (14½ in) in diameter and 127 mm (5 in) high. The wide flange is very sculptured and fluid as it blends into the body of the bowl and into the bead that frames the bowl's opening. A much larger burr oak bowl uses the natural spiky outer as a dramatic intervention in the underbelly and the flange edge of what is otherwise a very formal shape. This bowl is 508 mm (20 in) in diameter and 178 mm (7 in) high. It is also quite heavy to allow for the use of the spiky burr feature. Pieces like this are difficult to keep crisp in sanding, as there is always a tendency to soften the area around the void due to its intermittent passing at a slow speed. Good tool work will ensure minimal sanding, which should be done with great care, in order to keep the edges crisp.

Below: *Burr mulberry natural topped shell-like form bowl, 305 × 175 mm (12 × 7 in). Top right: Burr oak flanged bowl with natural edge 368 × 127 mm (14½ × 5 in). Bottom right: Large burr oak flanged bowl with natural burr feature through the flange and the understructure, 508 × 178 mm (20 × 7 in)*

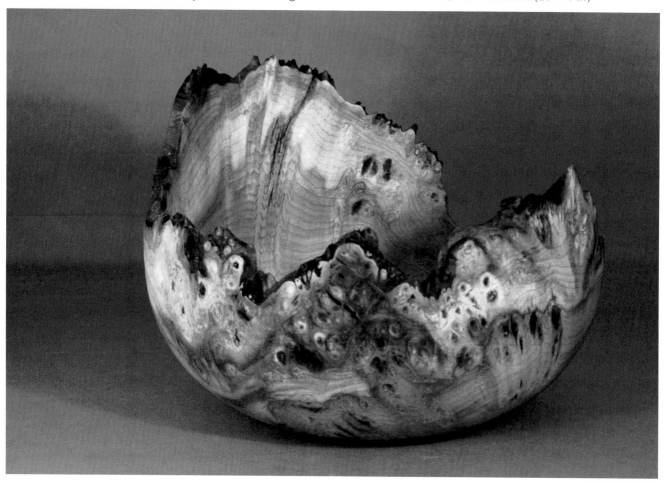

The elm burr bowl shows the total use of the burr for its understructure. The first person I ever saw use this feature was Tobias Kaye in the early 1980s. He left the burr totally natural. When the bowl was set down on a table it settled into what was its natural position, though he had taken care in his choice of material to make this as balanced as possible.

For my own work in this field I always use an inserted foot, which allows for a positive even seating. I usually paint them black (though this one is not) to make them as unobtrusive as possible, and to give the effect that the bowl is floating. A number of turners use other approaches – small inserted tripod feet; a hollow ring; or a flat foot, disc-sanded or planed on the bottom. I hate this last method. Unfortunately it is the most common, but is often left with screw holes showing. It may be an easy solution, but it looks awful and shows a lack of attention to detail that kills the whole thing.

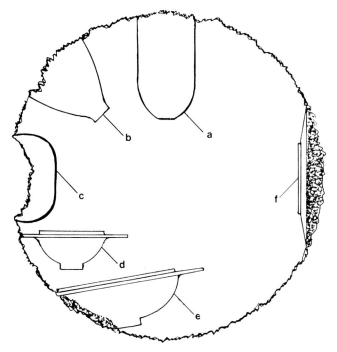

Above: *Illustration showing how the bowls on pages 102, 103, 104, 105 and 106 (a–f) were cut from a log. The oak bowls were all cut from the same log*

Below: *Burr elm bowl with full spiky burr understructure and inset foot, 400 × 75 mm (15¾ × 3 in)*

Conclusion

There is, I believe, in the woodturning world today, a more intense desire than ever before to create a strong personal identity for one's work. This is never easy, for most shapes will have been created at some time, but it should still be possible to bring a personal nuance to your work, be it through refinement or bold statement. If you think of the performing arts – be it ballet, opera, or Shakespeare – there are those who have the ability to put their own personal stamp on roles and make them their own, even though they have been performed countless times by others. So it is in the three-dimensional world of the arts and crafts. Only a few possess the ability to create such strong images that their work is recognized instantly, but the numbers are growing as more and more makers embark on the quest for a more personal identity within their work. The immense enjoyment that comes from turning wood is heightened still further when you start to create work with a strong personal stamp. The quest will not be easy, but is certainly worthwhile.

So, never be afraid to try new ideas. Keep an open mind, never become complacent – look, learn, and discover, explore your potential. Always strive to make the next piece better than the last. But most of all, enjoy what you do!

Typical signature pieces in walnut and lignum vitae (Ray Key)

Useful addresses

These organizations will be able to give you the contact names and addresses of local woodturning clubs in Britain, the USA, Canada, Australia and New Zealand.

THE ASSOCIATION OF WOODTURNERS OF GREAT BRITAIN
(Chairman Tony Waddilove)
11 St John Court
Swaffham
Norfolk PE37 7DB
UK
Publish 'Revolutions'

THE IRISH WOODTURNERS GUILD
17 Thornhill Heights
Celbridge
Co Kildare
Ireland
Publish a newsletter

ASSOCIATION OF AMERICAN WOODTURNERS
(Administrator Mary Reddig)
667 Harriet Avenue
Shoreview
MN 55126
USA
Publish 'American Woodturning'

CANADIAN WOODTURNERS ASSOCIATION
(Secretary Bob Stone)
5733 Atkins St
Gloucester
Ontario K1W 2V2
Canada
Publish 'Canadian Woodturner'

THE CRAFTS COUNCIL OF AUSTRALIA
100 George Street
Sydney
NSW 2000

(or contact the Crafts Council in the appropriate state)

WOODTURNERS GUILD OF NEW SOUTH WALES
21 Woodburn Avenue
Panania
NSW 2213

WOODTURNERS ASSOCIATION OF WESTERN AUSTRALIA
26 Norbury Crescent
City Beach
WA 6015

WOODTURNERS SOCIETY OF QUEENSLAND
19 Pine Street
Greenslopes
QLD 4120

NEW ZEALAND ASSOCIATION OF WOODTURNERS
P.O. Box 93
Fielding
New Zealand
Publish 'Faceplate'

In addition to the journals and magazines published by the national woodturning associations, articles on woodturning are published in all major woodwork magazines, often in crafts magazines, and also in the specialist woodturning magazines:

WOODTURNING
166 High Street
Lewes
East Sussex BN7 1XU
UK

THE WOODTURNER
The Mill
Millers Dale
Near Buxton
Derbyshire SK17 8SN

DRECHSELN
Martin Nolte
Im Winkel 14
4799 Borchen-Ettlen
Germany

Further reading

HOGBIN, Stephen, *Woodturning: The Purpose of the Object* Van Nostrand Reinold Co. Inc, New York (1980).

JACOBSON, Edward, *The Art of Turned Wooden Bowls*, E.P. Dutton Inc, New York (1985).

JAMES, Gerald T., *Woodturning: Design and Practice*, John Murray, London (1958).

KEY, Ray, *Woodturning and Design*, B.T. Batsford Ltd, London (1985). Published in the USA as *Woodturning: A Designer's Notebook* Sterling Publishing Co. Inc, New York (1987).

LINCOLN, William A., *World Woods in Colour*, Stobart and Son Ltd, London (1986).

LINDQUIST, Mark, *Sculpting Wood*: Davis Publications Inc, USA (1986).

NISH, Dale, *Master Woodturners*, Artisan Press, USA (1985).

PAIN, Frank, *The Practical Woodturner*, Evans Brothers, London (1957).

PYE, David, *The Nature and Aesthetics of Design*, The Herbert Press Ltd, London (1978).

PYE, David, *The Nature and Art of Workmanship*, Cambridge University Press, (1968).

PYE, David, *Wood Carver and Turner*, Crafts Council, London (1986).

RAFFAN, Richard, *Turned Bowl Design*, The Taunton Press Inc, USA (1987).

SEALE, Roland, *Practical Designs for Woodturning*, Evans Bros Ltd, London (1964).

Suppliers

AXMINSTER POWER TOOLS
Chard Street
Axminster
Devon
EX13 5DZ
England
Chucks and tools

FRANK BODDY'S
The Woodworkers Superstore
Riverside Sawmills
Boroughbridge
North Yorks
YO5 9LJ
England
All requirements plus wood

CRAFT SUPPLIES LTD
The Mill
Millers Dale
Nr Buxton
Derbyshire
SK17 8SN
England
All requirements plus wood

CRAFT SUPPLIES USA
1287 East 1120 South
Provo
UT 84601
USA
*All requirements including
Glaser tools & Robertson screws*

FIDDES & SON LTD
Florence Works
Brindley Road
Cardiff
CF1 7TX
South Wales
All finishing materials

GARRETT WADE CO. INC.
161 Avenue of the Americas
New York
NY 10013
USA
Tools and equipment

ALAN HOLTHAM
The Old Stores
Wistaston Road
Willaston
Nantwich
Cheshire
CW5 6QJ
England
All requirements plus wood

L.R.E. MACHINERY & EQ. CO.
15 Upwood Road
Lowton
Warrington
WA3 2RL
England
Lathes (new and reconditioned)

RACAL SAFETY LTD
Beresford Avenue
Wembley
Middlesex
HA0 1QJ
England
Air stream safety helmets

ROLSTON TIMBER
Hop Cottage
Worcester Road
Leigh Sinton
Malvern
Worcestershire
WR13 5EQ
England
Timber

WOODCRAFT SUPPLY
Wood Country Park
No 210 P.O. Box 1686
Parkersburg
WV 26101
USA
Tools and equipment

Index